2016

PENGU

FOUNDING EDIT
GENERAL EDITO
SUPERVISORY EDITORS: PAUL E.

HENRY V

T. J. B. SPENCER, sometime Director of the Shakespeare Institute of the University of Birmingham, was the founding editor of the New Penguin Shakespeare, for which he edited both *Romeo and Juliet* and *Hamlet*.

STANLEY WELLS is Honorary President of the Shakespeare Birthplace Trust, Emeritus Professor of Shakespeare Studies at the University of Birmingham, and General Editor of the Oxford Shakespeare. His many books include *Shakespeare: For All Time*, *Shakespeare & Co.*, *Shakespeare, Sex, and Love* and *Great Shakespeare Actors*.

A. R. HUMPHREYS was Professor of English at the University of Leicester. He edited *Julius Caesar* for the Oxford Shakespeare, *Much Ado About Nothing* and *King Henry IV, Parts I* and *II* for the Arden edition and *Henry VIII* for Penguin.

ANN KAEGI is Lecturer in English at the University of Hull. She has written on Shakespeare, the rhetoric of consensus, the dynamic of resistance, and the links between mourning and historical remembrance in early modern English drama.

WILLIAM SHAKESPEARE

Henry V

Edited with a Commentary by
A. R. HUMPHREYS
Revised and with an Introduction by
ANN KAEGI

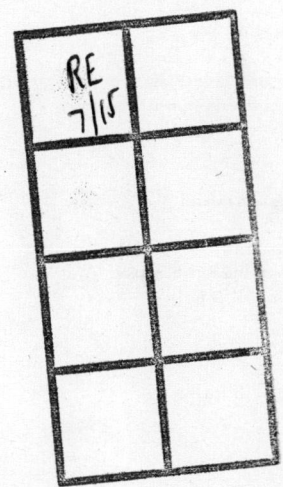

RE
7/15

PENGUIN BOOKS

PENGUIN CLASSICS

UK | USA | Canada | Ireland | Australia
India | New Zealand | South Africa

Penguin Books is part of the Penguin Random House group of companies
whose addresses can be found at global.penguinrandomhouse.com.

This edition first published in Penguin Books 1968
Reissued in the Penguin Shakespeare series 2010
Reissued in Penguin Classics 2015

001

Set in Postscript Monotype Fournier
Typeset by Palimpsest Book Production Limited, Falkirk, Stirlingshire
Printed in Great Britain by Clays Ltd, St Ives plc

ISBN: 978-0-141-39667-5

Contents

General Introduction

Every play by Shakespeare is unique. This is part of his greatness. A restless and indefatigable experimenter, he moved with a rare amalgamation of artistic integrity and dedicated professionalism from one kind of drama to another. Never shackled by convention, he offered his actors the alternation between serious and comic modes from play to play, and often also within the plays themselves, that the repertory system within which he worked demanded, and which provided an invaluable stimulus to his imagination. Introductions to individual works in this series attempt to define their individuality. But there are common factors that underpin Shakespeare's career.

Nothing in his heredity offers clues to the origins of his genius. His upbringing in Stratford-upon-Avon, where he was born in 1564, was unexceptional. His mother, born Mary Arden, came from a prosperous farming family. Her father chose her as his executor over her eight sisters and his four stepchildren when she was only in her late teens, which suggests that she was of more than average practical ability. Her husband John, a glover, apparently unable to write, was nevertheless a capable businessman and loyal townsfellow, who seems to have fallen on relatively hard times in later life. He would have been brought up as a Catholic, and may have retained

Catholic sympathies, but his son subscribed publicly to Anglicanism throughout his life.

The most important formative influence on Shakespeare was his school. As the son of an alderman who became bailiff (or mayor) in 1568, he had the right to attend the town's grammar school. Here he would have received an education grounded in classical rhetoric and oratory, studying authors such as Ovid, Cicero and Quintilian, and would have been required to read, speak, write and even think in Latin from his early years. This classical education permeates Shakespeare's work from the beginning to the end of his career. It is apparent in the self-conscious classicism of plays of the early 1590s such as the tragedy of *Titus Andronicus*, *The Comedy of Errors*, and the narrative poems *Venus and Adonis* (1592–3) and *The Rape of Lucrece* (1593–4), and is still evident in his latest plays, informing the dream visions of *Pericles* and *Cymbeline* and the masque in *The Tempest*, written between 1607 and 1611. It inflects his literary style throughout his career. In his earliest writings the verse, based on the ten-syllabled, five-beat iambic pentameter, is highly patterned. Rhetorical devices deriving from classical literature, such as alliteration and antithesis, extended similes and elaborate wordplay, abound. Often, as in *Love's Labour's Lost* and *A Midsummer Night's Dream*, he uses rhyming patterns associated with lyric poetry, each line self-contained in sense, the prose as well as the verse employing elaborate figures of speech. Writing at a time of linguistic ferment, Shakespeare frequently imports Latinisms into English, coining words such as abstemious, addiction, incarnadine and adjunct. He was also heavily influenced by the eloquent translations of the Bible in both the Bishops' and the Geneva versions. As his experience grows, his verse and prose become more supple, the patterning less apparent, more ready to accommodate the rhythms of ordinary speech, more colloquial in diction, as in the speeches of the Nurse in *Romeo and Juliet*, the characterful prose of Falstaff, and Hamlet's soliloquies. The effect is of increasing psychological realism, reaching its greatest heights in *Hamlet*, *Othello*, *King Lear*, *Macbeth* and *Antony and Cleopatra*. Gradually he discovered ways of adapting the regular beat of the pentameter to make it an infinitely flexible instrument for matching thought with feeling. Towards the end of his career, in plays such as *The Winter's Tale*, *Cymbeline* and *The Tempest*, he adopts a more highly mannered style, in keeping with the more overtly symbolical and emblematical mode in which he is writing.

So far as we know, Shakespeare lived in Stratford till after his marriage to Anne Hathaway, eight years his senior, in 1582. They had three children: a daughter, Susanna, born in 1583 within six months of their marriage, and twins, Hamnet and Judith, born in 1585. The next seven years of Shakespeare's life are virtually a blank. Theories that he may have been, for instance, a schoolmaster, or a lawyer, or a soldier, or a sailor, lack evidence to support them. The first reference to him in print, in Robert Greene's pamphlet *Greene's Groatsworth of Wit* of 1592, parodies a line from *Henry VI, Part III*, implying that Shakespeare was already an established playwright. It seems likely that at some unknown point after the birth of his twins he joined a theatre company and gained experience as both actor and writer in the provinces and London. The London theatres closed because of plague in 1593 and 1594; and during these years, perhaps recognizing the need for an alternative career, he wrote and published the narrative poems *Venus and Adonis* and *The Rape of Lucrece*. These are the only works we can be certain that Shakespeare himself was responsible for putting into print. Each bears the author's dedication to Henry Wriothesley, Earl of Southampton (1573–1624), the second in warmer terms than the first. Southampton, younger than Shakespeare by ten years, is the only person to whom he personally dedicated works. The Earl may have been a close friend, perhaps even the beautiful and adored young man whom Shakespeare celebrates in his *Sonnets*.

The resumption of playing after the plague years saw the founding of the Lord Chamberlain's Men, a company to which Shakespeare was to belong for the rest of his career, as actor, shareholder and playwright. No other dramatist of the period had so stable a relationship with a single company. Shakespeare knew the actors for whom he was writing and the conditions in which they performed. The permanent company was made up of around twelve to fourteen players, but one actor often played more than one role in a play and additional actors were hired as needed. Led by the tragedian Richard Burbage (1568–1619) and, initially, the comic actor Will Kemp (d. 1603), they rapidly achieved a high reputation, and when King James I succeeded Queen Elizabeth I in 1603 they were renamed as the King's Men. All the women's parts were played by boys; there is no evidence that any female role was ever played by a male actor over the age of about eighteen. Shakespeare had enough confidence in his boys to write for them long and demanding roles such as Rosalind (who, like other heroines of the romantic comedies, is disguised as a boy for much of the action) in *As You Like It*, Lady Macbeth and Cleopatra. But there are far more fathers than mothers, sons than daughters, in his plays, few if any of which require more than the company's normal complement of three or four boys.

The company played primarily in London's public playhouses – there were almost none that we know of in the rest of the country – initially in the Theatre, built in Shoreditch in 1576, and from 1599 in the Globe, on Bankside. These were wooden, more or less circular structures, open to the air, with a thrust stage surmounted by a canopy and jutting into the area where spectators who paid one penny stood, and surrounded by galleries where it was possible to be seated on payment of an additional penny. Though properties such as cauldrons, stocks, artificial trees or beds could indicate locality, there was no representational scenery. Sound effects such as flourishes of trumpets, music both martial and amorous, and accompaniments to songs were provided by the company's musicians. Actors entered through doors in the back wall of the stage. Above it was a balconied area that could represent the walls of a town (as in *King John*), or a castle (as in *Richard II*), and indeed a balcony (as in *Romeo and Juliet*). In 1609 the company also acquired the use of the Blackfriars, a smaller, indoor theatre to which admission was more expensive, and which permitted the use of more spectacular stage effects such as the descent of Jupiter on an eagle in *Cymbeline* and of goddesses in *The Tempest*. And they would frequently perform before the court in royal residences and, on their regular tours into the provinces, in non-theatrical spaces such as inns, guildhalls and the great halls of country houses.

Early in his career Shakespeare may have worked in collaboration, perhaps with Thomas Nashe (1567–*c.* 1601) in *Henry VI, Part I* and with George Peele (1556–96) in *Titus Andronicus*. And towards the end he collaborated with George Wilkins (*fl.* 1604–8) in *Pericles*, and with his younger colleagues Thomas Middleton (1580–1627), in *Timon of Athens*, and John Fletcher (1579–1625), in *Henry*

VIII, *The Two Noble Kinsmen* and the lost play *Cardenio*. Shakespeare's output dwindled in his last years, and he died in 1616 in Stratford, where he owned a fine house, New Place, and much land. His only son had died at the age of eleven, in 1596, and his last descendant died in 1670. New Place was destroyed in the eighteenth century but the other Stratford houses associated with his life are maintained and displayed to the public by the Shakespeare Birthplace Trust.

One of the most remarkable features of Shakespeare's plays is their intellectual and emotional scope. They span a great range from the lightest of comedies, such as *The Two Gentlemen of Verona* and *The Comedy of Errors*, to the profoundest of tragedies, such as *King Lear* and *Macbeth*. He maintained an output of around two plays a year, ringing the changes between comic and serious. All his comedies have serious elements: Shylock, in *The Merchant of Venice*, almost reaches tragic dimensions, and *Measure for Measure* is profoundly serious in its examination of moral problems. Equally, none of his tragedies is without humour: Hamlet is as witty as any of his comic heroes, *Macbeth* has its Porter, and *King Lear* its Fool. His greatest comic character, Falstaff, inhabits the history plays and *Henry V* ends with a marriage, while *Henry VI, Part III*, *Richard II* and *Richard III* culminate in the tragic deaths of their protagonists.

Although in performance Shakespeare's characters can give the impression of a superabundant reality, he is not a naturalistic dramatist. None of his plays is explicitly set in his own time. The action of few of them (except for the English histories) is set even partly in England (exceptions are *The Merry Wives of Windsor* and the Induction to *The Taming of the Shrew*). Italy is his favoured location. Most of his principal story-lines derive from printed writings; but the structuring and translation of these narratives into dramatic terms is Shakespeare's own, and he invents much additional material. Most of the plays contain elements of myth and legend, and many derive from ancient or more recent history or from romantic tales of ancient times and faraway places. All reflect his reading, often in close detail. Holinshed's *Chronicles* (1577, revised 1587), a great compendium of English, Scottish and Irish history, provided material for his English history plays. The *Lives of the Noble Grecians and Romans* by the Greek writer Plutarch, finely translated into English from the French by Sir Thomas North in 1579, provided much of the narrative material, and also a mass of verbal detail, for his plays about Roman history. Some plays are closely based on shorter individual works: *As You Like It*, for instance, on the novel *Rosalynde* (1590) by his near-contemporary Thomas Lodge (1558–1625), *The Winter's Tale* on *Pandosto* (1588) by his old rival Robert Greene (1558–92) and *Othello* on a story by the Italian Giraldi Cinthio (1504–73). And the language of his plays is permeated by the Bible, the Book of Common Prayer and the proverbial sayings of his day.

Shakespeare was popular with his contemporaries, but his commitment to the theatre and to the plays in performance is demonstrated by the fact that only about half of his plays appeared in print in his lifetime, in slim paperback volumes known as quartos, so called because they were made from printers' sheets folded twice to form four leaves (eight pages). None of them shows any sign that he was involved in their publication. For him, performance was the primary means of publication. The most frequently reprinted of his works were the non-dramatic poems – the erotic *Venus and Adonis* and the more moralistic *The Rape of Lucrece*. The *Sonnets*, which appeared in 1609, under his name but possibly without his consent, were less successful, perhaps because the vogue for sonnet sequences, which peaked in the 1590s, had passed by then. They were not reprinted until 1640, and then only in garbled form along with poems by other writers. Happily, in 1623, seven years after he died, his colleagues John Heminges (1556–1630) and Henry Condell (d. 1627) published his collected plays, including eighteen that had not previously appeared in print, in the first Folio, whose name derives from the fact that the printers' sheets were folded only once to produce two leaves (four pages). Some of the quarto editions are badly printed, and the fact that some plays exist in two, or even three, early versions creates problems for editors. These are discussed in the Account of the Text in each volume of this series.

Shakespeare's plays continued in the repertoire until the Puritans closed the theatres in 1642. When performances resumed after the Restoration of the monarchy in 1660, many of the plays were not to the taste of the times, especially because their mingling of genres and failure to meet the requirements of poetic justice offended against the dictates of neoclassicism. Some, such as *The Tempest* (changed by John Dryden and William Davenant in 1667 to suit contemporary taste), *King Lear* (to which Nahum Tate gave a happy ending in 1681) and *Richard III* (heavily adapted by Colley Cibber in 1700 as a vehicle for his own talents), were extensively rewritten; others fell into neglect. Slowly they regained their place in the repertoire, and they continued to be reprinted, but it was not until the great actor David Garrick (1717–79) organized a spectacular jubilee in Stratford in 1769 that Shakespeare began to be regarded as a transcendental genius. Garrick's idolatry prefigured the enthusiasm of critics such as Samuel Taylor Coleridge (1772–1834) and William Hazlitt (1778–1830). Gradually Shakespeare's reputation spread abroad, to Germany, America, France and to other European countries.

During the nineteenth century, though the plays were generally still performed in heavily adapted or abbreviated versions, a large body of scholarship and criticism began to amass. Partly as a result of a general swing in education away from the teaching of Greek and Roman texts and towards literature written in English, Shakespeare became the object of intensive study in schools and universities. In the theatre, important turning points were the work in England of two theatre directors, William Poel (1852–1934) and his disciple Harley Granville-Barker (1877–1946), who showed that the application of knowledge, some of it newly acquired, of early staging conditions to performance of the plays could render the original texts viable in terms of the modern theatre. During the twentieth century appreciation of Shakespeare's work, encouraged by the availability of audio, film and video versions of the plays, spread around the world to such an extent that he can now be claimed as a global author.

The influence of Shakespeare's works permeates the English language. Phrases from his plays and poems – 'a tower of strength', 'green-eyed jealousy', 'a foregone conclusion' – are on the lips of people who may never have read him. They have inspired composers of songs, orchestral music and operas; painters and sculptors; poets, novelists and film-makers. Allusions to him appear in pop songs, in advertisements and in television shows. Some of his characters – Romeo and Juliet, Falstaff, Shylock and Hamlet – have acquired mythic status. He is valued for his humanity, his psychological insight, his wit and humour, his lyricism, his mastery of language, his ability to excite, surprise, move and, in the widest sense of the word, entertain audiences. He is the greatest of poets, but he is essentially a dramatic poet. Though his plays have much to offer to readers, they exist fully only in performance. In these volumes we offer individual introductions, notes on language and on specific points of the text, suggestions for further reading and information about how each work has been edited. In addition we include accounts of the ways in which successive generations of interpreters and audiences have responded to challenges and rewards offered by the plays. The Penguin Shakespeare series aspires to remove obstacles to understanding and to make pleasurable the reading of the work of the man who has done more than most to make us understand what it is to be human.

Stanley Wells

The Chronology of Shakespeare's Works

A few of Shakespeare's writings can be fairly precisely dated. An allusion to the Earl of Essex in the chorus to Act V of *Henry V*, for instance, could only have been written in 1599. But for many of the plays we have only vague information, such as the date of publication, which may have occurred long after composition, the date of a performance, which may not have been the first, or a list in Francis Meres's book *Palladis Tamia*, published in 1598, which tells us only that the plays listed there must have been written by that year. The chronology of the early plays is particularly difficult to establish. Not everyone would agree that the first part of *Henry VI* was written after the third, for instance, or *Romeo and Juliet* before *A Midsummer Night's Dream*. The following table is based on the 'Canon and Chronology' section in *William Shakespeare: A Textual Companion*, by Stanley Wells and Gary Taylor, with John Jowett and William Montgomery (1987), where more detailed information and discussion may be found.

The Two Gentlemen of Verona	1590–91
The Taming of the Shrew	1590–91
Henry VI, Part II	1591
Henry VI, Part III	1591

Introduction

Shakespeare's *Henry V* can seem at once impossibly remote and eerily familiar. This dual impression is not unique to *Henry V* nor is it limited to Shakespeare's historical dramas, but it is one to which they are particularly susceptible due to their distinctive mix of historic personages and events, on the one hand, and enduring struggles for power on the other. The serial topicality of *Henry V* is among its most striking features. In Shakespeare's day persistent threats of invasion by Spain and intensifying conflict in Ireland gave added resonance to plays about England's illustrious warrior king and his stunning victory at Agincourt. The performance history of *Henry V* has been closely tied to the fortunes of war, yet what sets Shakespeare's play apart from other contemporary plays featuring celebrated battles is not so much its depiction of war as the arresting manner in which it both exploits and exposes the power of speech to persuade. The fashioning of speech into a sophisticated political, military and theatrical instrument, an instrument of power, is a hallmark of the play and marks the emergence in *Henry V* of a challenging form of political drama in which audiences are subjected to competing and incompatible claims by successive speakers that put our judgement to the test.

The suggestion that what distinguishes *Henry V* is not

so much its anatomy of war as its anatomy of the power of persuasion may seem odd, as it is often described as Shakespeare's war play and has frequently been performed and twice filmed at times of war or in the aftermath of military conflict. Yet there are as many battle scenes in *Henry IV, Part I*, and considerably more in the *Henry VI* plays. Unless additional business has been devised, the closest audiences come to witnessing a major battle scene in *Henry V* is the second assault on Harfleur, an attack that the town's defenders successfully repulse. As for the famed battle of Agincourt, apart from the sound of several military signals (IV.4.0, IV.5.5, IV.6.0, 34, IV.7.52) and one stage direction calling for '*Excursions*' (military skirmishes or sorties across the stage; IV.4.0), the only sustained military engagement we witness is an anticlimactic encounter between two misapprehending cowards: the terrified Monsieur Le Fer and the bombastic Pistol – just the sort of 'brawl ridiculous' (IV.Chorus.51) from which the Chorus seeks to distract us with stirring words. In marked contrast to *Henry IV, Part I*, where he shows courage by fulfilling his pledge to kill the intrepid Hotspur 'in single fight' (V.1.96–100), in *Henry V* we never see Henry engage in single combat with an esteemed martial adversary. Yet unlike the King of France, who delegates command on the battlefield to the Constable, Henry risks his life by leading his army into battle at Harfleur and again at Agincourt, where, faced with overwhelming odds, he spurns repeated offers of ransom. In so doing Henry V outdoes his famous ancestor King Edward III, who surveyed the clash of armies at Crécy from a nearby hill while his son Edward, the Black Prince, 'played a tragedy, | Making defeat on the full power of France' (I.2.106–7). At Agincourt, however, the only military command we hear Henry utter, aside from his instructions to the English

Herald, is his chilling order to kill defenceless French prisoners (IV.6.37, IV.7.61). If we believe we have witnessed
the re-enactment of an epic conflict, that is either because
the Chorus has conjured up a vivid impression of the clash
of armies in our minds or because elaborate battle scenes
have been devised for performance. That *Henry V* should
be known as Shakespeare's war play when it contains relatively few scenes of combat, and those few are at odds
with the stuff of legend and the Chorus's rousing account
of an epic struggle, is one of many paradoxes that mark
the play's reception.

However, it is neither for its evocation of battle nor
for its cogent exploration of the motives for, prosecution
of and political capital to be made from war that the play
advances its most pressing claim for continued attention.
Henry V remains an important and compelling drama
above all because of its enduring and unrivalled capacity
to test our desire to remember, our inclination to
forget and our openness to persuasion. In *Hamlet* we listen
to the prince ponder the ethics of revenge. In *Henry V*
it is we the audience who are directly urged to 'Work,
work . . . [our] thoughts' (III.Chorus.25) while simultaneously being encouraged to abandon judgement, yield
unthinkingly to the enticing oratory of the King and his
Chorus on a matter of war and 'Follow, follow!' (17).
Unless we remain vigilant we risk being 'marvellously
mistook' (III.6.79), as our capacity to remember and
willingness to forget are probed at every turn. With
the possible exception of *Julius Caesar*, no other
Shakespearian play brings home so forcefully, and not
even *Julius Caesar* brings home as insistently, the political value of controlling how the past is remembered and
the relative ease with which historical remembrance can
be manipulated for political ends.

The refashioning of the past into a patriotic epic and so into political myth is the principal function of the choruses, beginning with the Prologue's comparison of 'warlike Harry' (5) to the Roman god of war and concluding with the Epilogue's memorial sonnet to 'This star of England' (6). But the version of history promoted in the choruses proves unreliable. Even as we are encouraged by the Chorus to respond unthinkingly to its rousing account of Henry V's wars in France, the dramatic sequence prompts us to note the difference between what we hear and what we see and to recall the actual as distinct from the (mis)reported sequence of events. Meanwhile, the play's inclusion of dissonant voices – the Eastcheapers, the conspirators, the quarrelsome captains, the common soldiers, Burgundy and Katherine – opens up alternative versions of history to the official version sponsored by the Chorus. While the famous victories of Henry V are central to Shakespeare's historical drama, the need to exercise discernment in responding to a play of persuasion that draws audiences one way and then another on a matter of war lies at the heart of Shakespeare's testing theatre of judgement. For much of its performance history the latter has been sacrificed in favour of a version of the former modelled on the choruses, resulting in a potentially stirring but comparatively slight drama. *Henry V*, its audiences and our times deserve better.

THE TWO VERSIONS OF *HENRY V* AND THE CLIMATE OF WAR

Henry V depicts a military expedition against a country that is an irritant but does not pose an imminent threat to the invading power. The ensuing conflict causes the invaded land, formerly 'this best garden of the world' (V.2.36), to 'grow to wildness' (55) and its people to 'grow like savages' (59). Perhaps it is unsurprising that it has proved the most critically divisive of Shakespeare's plays in modern times. Changing attitudes to war, and especially to military invasions of dubious warrant, have contributed to this modern critical phenomenon, but the emergence of opposing responses to *Henry V* is also bound up with the way it arouses expectations one moment and upsets them the next. The existence of two very different surviving early versions of *Henry V*, one exceptionally short and the other unusually long, raises the intriguing possibility that Shakespeare's play may also have divided its earliest interpreters. Most modern editions of *Henry V*, including the present one, are based on *The Life of Henry the Fifth*, the version included in the first collected edition of Shakespeare's plays, now commonly known as the first Folio, which was compiled by two of Shakespeare's former fellow actors, John Heminges and Henry Condell, and printed posthumously in 1623. A very different version of *Henry V* was issued as a quarto in August 1600, bearing the descriptive title *The Chronicle History of Henry the Fifth, with His Battle Fought at Agincourt in France. Together with Ancient Pistol.* Although *The Chronicle History* (known as the first Quarto) was the only version printed in Shakespeare's lifetime, his name is notably absent from its title page, the only one of five Shakespeare plays printed that year not to record Shakespeare's authorship. Its title page purports to offer the play 'As it hath been sundry times played' by the Lord Chamberlain's Men (the playing company of which Shakespeare became a principal shareholder in 1599); however, this claim and Shakespeare's direct involvement in devising the acting script from which *The*

Chronicle History supposedly derives remain in doubt (see 'Textual Issues' in Further Reading).

The two versions are distinguished not only by their sharply differing lengths (*The Chronicle History* is half the length of *The Life*) but also by their divergent representations of Henry V and his French campaign. *The Chronicle History* omits all of the choruses (including the Prologue and Epilogue), removes or truncates the longest speeches, leaves out entire scenes and transposes others, reduces the number of roles and makes consistent changes to names (the most notable being the elimination of the Dauphin from Agincourt through the reassignment of his speeches to Bourbon). The representation of Henry V, the motives for and conduct of his war are transformed by the omission of Act I, scene 1 and lines 115–35 of Act I, scene 2, removing any hint of a financial motive for Canterbury's interpretation of the Salic law and the bishops' eagerness to sanction – and fund – Henry's war; any suggestion in Act II, scene 1 that Henry is responsible for Falstaff's death; Cambridge's hint that deeper motives than bribery prompted him to join the conspiracy (II.2.155–60); Jamy, Macmorris and the quarrel over Macmorris's 'nation' in Act III, scene 2; most of the Harfleur episode, including Henry's famous rallying speech (III.1) together with his most savage threats to the townspeople (III.3.11–41); much of Henry's disquieting exchange with his soldiers on the night before Agincourt in Act IV, scene 1; the lengthy section of Henry's soliloquy on ceremony and the burdens of kingship (IV.1.223–77); any mention of the hanging of Nym (IV.4.68–71); the whole of Burgundy's evocative description of the havoc caused by Henry's invasion (V.2.34–67); much of the dialogue between Henry and Princess Katherine; and the edgy sexual banter between Burgundy and Henry (V.2.277–322) – material crucial to Henry's characterization. The 'short' version thus dispenses with much of the material that detracts from a straightforwardly heroic and patriotic account of Henry V and his French wars, resulting in a pacier, more jingoistic and considerably more orthodox play. The 'long' and 'short' versions of *Henry V* are thus not merely distinct but potentially opposing. Many argue that *The Chronicle History* supplies the idealized heroic and patriotic war play that some have taken *The Life* to be.

Shakespeare's unsettling account of a celebrated English king and his French wars in the 'long' Folio version of *Henry V* appears all the more daring if we reflect on the historical circumstances in which the playwright devised his heterodox drama. The play was (most probably) written and first performed in 1599, the last year of a tumultuous century and at the end of the most militarist decade in Elizabethan history, during which time people in England lived in fear of imminent invasion by Spain. The failure of the 'Glorious Armada' of 1588 did not end fears of a Spanish naval assault. Rapid Spanish rearmament meant that the threat of invasion persisted, with further invasion scares over the next decade and annually from 1596 (the year the port of Calais fell to Spain) until 1599 prompting sudden mobilizations of men and shipping to strengthen England's defences followed by their abrupt disbandment when the rumours of an armada proved false or severe storms scattered the Spanish fleet. Forced musters of men became a regular occurrence, and trained bands of citizen militia were frequently to be seen performing military drills on London fields and in provincial churchyards.

War and the threat of invasion shaped late-Elizabethan

culture and influenced Shakespeare's theatre of war in
Henry V in myriad ways. 'Art of war' writing prolifer-
ated, particularly manuals on the orderly conduct of war
and the attributes of an ideal general, generating an enter-
tainingly quarrelsome battle as rival captains vehemently
denounced one another's theories in print (Jorgensen,
Shakespeare's Military World, pp. 72–3). Shakespeare
gently mocks the appetite for such literature and the argu-
mentative character of the Elizabethan manual debate in
the person of Captain Fluellen. A fiercely loyal Welshman
with a temperament as 'hot as gunpowder' (IV.7.175),
Fluellen nonetheless allows his fondness for 'disputations
... touching or concerning the disciplines of the war'
(III.2.92–4) to get in the way of the fighting during the
heat of the battle for Harfleur, much to the annoyance
of Captain Macmorris, who notes that 'it is no time to
discourse, ... there is throats to be cut, and works to be
done' (104–9). Fluellen's comically pedantic obsession
with 'the disciplines of the pristine wars of the Romans'
(79) parodies the advice to study the 'ancient Roman disciplines for the wars ... and accommodate them to the
service of our time' (Preface, pp. Aiii^v–Aiv^r) offered by
Leonard and Thomas Digges in their influential guide to
military tactics *An Arithmeticall Militare Treatise, Named
Stratioticos* (1579), a book that Shakespeare may have
come upon when it was reissued in 1590 by his fellow
Stratfordian Richard Field (who printed Shakespeare's
Venus and Adonis in 1593).

While London's bookstalls filled up with war manuals,
war plays were in vogue in its playhouses. Christopher
Marlowe set the pattern with his ground-breaking
conqueror play *Tamburlaine the Great* (*c*. 1587–8), which
proved so popular that he promptly wrote a sequel (*c*.
1588). In devising his own conqueror play just over a

decade later, Shakespeare repeatedly summons up remembrance of Marlowe's seminal two-part drama: Pistol's bombastic speeches parody the 'high astounding terms' of Marlowe's Scythian shepherd (*Part One*, Prologue, l. 5); Henry's threatening speech at Harfleur recalls the threat of total war levelled by Tamburlaine at the siege of Damascus, only to distinguish Henry's instruction to 'Use mercy' (III.3.54) after Harfleur surrenders from Tamburlaine's order to put the citizens of Damascus 'to the sword' (*Part One*, V.1.134); and Henry's betrothal to Princess Katherine, his 'capital demand' (V.2.96) in the peace negotiations with France, has disturbing parallels with Tamburlaine's rape of and subsequent marriage to Zenocrate, daughter of the Sultan of Egypt. Several of the playhouses in which 1590s war plays were regularly performed were sited near the city's wartime training grounds (de Somogyi, *Shakespeare's Theatre of War*, pp. 124–6), including two, the Theatre and the Curtain, that have strong Shakespearian connections, the former as the home of Shakespeare's playing company until they built the Globe Theatre on Bankside in 1599 and the latter as the company's temporary home during the Globe's construction and quite possibly the 'wooden O' (Prologue.13) in which *Henry V* was first performed. Playgoers travelling to the first production of *Henry V* may well have passed within sight of actual soldiers rehearsing for battle in nearby fields. There is also evidence to suggest that captains and soldiers made up a significant portion of theatre audiences during this period (see R. B. McKerrow (ed.), *The Works of Thomas Nashe* (1904–10), vol. 1, p. 212). All of these factors would have lent a sense of immediacy to performances of war plays such as *Henry V* irrespective of their historically remote settings.

Several features of *Henry V* would have made its temporal setting seem considerably less remote in 1599. Contemporary wartime anxieties account for the presence in *Henry V* of material that is often omitted in modern performances yet would have blurred the boundary between past and present for the play's first audiences. Continuing fears of a Spanish armada may have prompted Shakespeare's choice of a maritime metaphor when Henry recounts how, when Edward III was waging war in France, 'the Scot on his unfurnished kingdom | Came pouring, like the tide into a breach' (I.2.148–9). Henry's preoccupation with the 'ill neighbourhood' of Scotland (136–221) also would have struck a chord after Elizabeth I's agents uncovered successive plots by Catholic earls in Scotland to join in league with Spain in the post-Armada years, and after the discovery in the 1590s that a number of Scottish nobles were fuelling revolt in Ireland. The lengthy debate by Henry and his war council over the threat of incursion posed by the Scots is now frequently omitted; however, inveterate distrust of England's 'giddy neighbour' (145) to the north and prevailing concerns about the need for England to protect itself from invasion by Spain while simultaneously fighting defensive wars abroad would have made this discussion of homeland security highly topical in 1599. In August 1599, just months after Elizabeth had sent over into Ireland the largest army to have been dispatched abroad since the reign of Henry VIII, England was plunged into its largest invasion scare since 1588. False reports that the Spanish had landed on the Isle of Wight caused panicked scenes in London as heavy chains were drawn across the Thames and the city's thoroughfares to hinder the rumoured invaders. As outlined below, Shakespeare probably wrote *Henry V* sometime between

February and September 1599, with the spring or early summer the most likely date of completion. If so, the debate about homeland defence in *Henry V* could not have been more timely.

While Elizabeth's testy relations with Scotland can be detected behind the protracted ruminations on 'the main intendment of the Scot' (I.2.144) by Henry's war council, the impact of Elizabeth's widening wars in Ireland on Shakespeare's account of Henry V's wars in France is more far-reaching and more diffuse. *Henry V* was written at the height of the Nine Years War in Ireland (1594–1603). The shift to open and sustained warfare in Ireland came less than a year before Shakespeare wrote *Henry V*, after an English force several thousand strong was slaughtered by Irish rebels in August 1598 and the Munster Plantation (a colony of 'New English' settlers) was overrun two months later. Ireland was Elizabeth's second kingdom; Spain viewed it as England's Achilles' heel and began supplying money, munitions and eventually also soldiers to support the revolt so as to threaten England with encirclement. To counter that menace and suppress the uprising, record numbers of Englishmen were hastily conscripted into military service at the end of 1598 and the first six months of 1599. This crisis in Irish affairs lies behind the repeated intrusion of Ireland into *Henry V*, a play set during Henry V's campaigns (1414–22) in the Hundred Years War (1337–1453) between England and France, fought more than a century before Henry VIII became the first English king to assume the title King of Ireland in the 1540s. The period of Lancastrian rule under Henry V and Henry VI acquired new meaning with the outbreak of open war in Ireland. Where the prospect of possessing forfeited 'rebel' lands in Munster and establishing themselves as landed gentry had offered New

English adventurers an opportunity unseen on such a scale since the time of Henry V and his conquests in France (MacCaffrey, *Elizabeth I*, p. 344), so the loss of the Munster colony called to mind the loss of England's possessions in France in the last phase of the Hundred Years War. The descriptions of Henry's '*poor soldiers*' (III.6.84) closely chime with Elizabethan reports of the famished nakedness of the poorly provisioned, disease-ridden (III.5.57, III.6.153, III.7.148, IV.2.14) and ill-shod (IV.8.68–71) royal army in Ireland. The unusually explicit topical reference in the fifth chorus to 'the General of our gracious Empress . . . from Ireland coming' (30–31); the inclusion of Macmorris; and other curious references to Ireland in the play, such as the cluster of mocking references to 'a kern of Ireland' (III.7.51), 'strait strossers' (52) and 'foul bogs' (55); Pistol's mispronunciation of an Irish ballad refrain, '*Calen o custure me!*' (IV.4.4); the anachronistic greeting, 'brother Ireland', Isabel addresses to Henry (see note to V.2.12); and Henry's equally anachronistic pledge to Katherine, 'England is thine, *Ireland is thine*, France is thine' (V.2.236–7; added emphasis) would have encouraged the play's first audiences to draw analogies between Henry V's wars in France and the ongoing wars in Ireland and, more narrowly, between the victor at Agincourt and the general whose triumphal return 'from Ireland' is anticipated in the fifth chorus (though whether these comparisons were favourable is open to question). The general alluded to is almost certainly Robert Devereux, the second Earl of Essex, whom Elizabeth had dispatched to Ireland in March 1599.

The thinly veiled reference to Essex makes it possible to date *Henry V* with unusual confidence to the period between February and September 1599 with internal evidence pointing to the spring or early summer as the most likely date of completion. After months of stalling Essex had finally accepted the Irish commission in February 1599. An ardent militarist, acclaimed 'Great England's glory and the world's wide wonder' by Edmund Spenser (*Prothalamion* (1596), l. 146), Essex had captured the public's imagination with his exploits at Rouen, Lisbon, Cadiz and the Azores. He left for Ireland on 27 March, cheered on by crowds of Londoners (John Stow, *Annales* (1615), pp. 787–8) confident that their popular hero would return 'Bringing rebellion broachèd on his sword' (V.Chorus.32). Contrary to popular expectations, Essex returned unauthorized to England on 28 September, having concluded a humiliating truce without Elizabeth's permission. Forty-eight hours later Essex was under house arrest. However, it had already become apparent by July that Essex's campaign might end in failure. If the play was written in the spring or early summer, the Chorus's unfavourable comparison of the popular support for Essex (characterized as 'lower', V. Chorus.29) to that merited by Henry V – 'Much more, and *much more cause*, | Did they this Harry' (34–5; added emphasis) – was prescient. Its use of the ambiguous phrase 'Bringing rebellion broachèd on his sword' (see note) allows for the possibility that Essex's return to the capital might threaten 'the peaceful city' (33) (Patterson, *Shakespeare and the Popular Voice*, pp. 84–7). And so it proved when on 8 February 1601 Essex attempted to launch a popular uprising in London in a bid to depose his rivals at court. Ill-conceived and clumsily executed, the attempted coup proved an abject failure: in rapid order Essex was captured, tried and beheaded.

CHRONICLING ENGLAND

It was in this wartime climate that the English history play emerged to become one of the dominant genres of the Elizabethan stage, and Shakespeare was at the fore-front of its invention. Historical writing had long been among the favourite reading matter of England's book-buying population. When William Caxton established the first printing press in England in 1476 one of the first books he printed was *The Chronicles of England* (1480). Designed for a lay readership, *Caxton's Chronicles* (as it came to be known) would go through thirteen printings in fifty years. The break with Rome under Henry VIII gave impetus to the task of writing England, its history, institutions, land and language; however, it was during the reign of Elizabeth I that the project of writing the English 'nation' into being reached fruition. Elizabeth's war years sharply heightened patriotic interest in the history of England and of London, its burgeoning capital, and a glut of histories issued from the presses. English history plays complemented, supplemented and, for those unable to read, substituted for these multiplying volumes of printed history. Many playgoers in Shakespeare's day and after derived their knowledge of England's past from stage plays. In his *Apology for Actors* (1612) Thomas Heywood maintained that history plays had so widely 'instructed such as cannot read in the discovery of all our English chronicles' that scarcely anyone 'cannot discourse of any notable thing recorded' (F3^r). The growing body of writing on the history of England helped to fashion a distinctive sense of 'Englishness'; in so doing it helped to generate (in Benedict Anderson's phrase) the 'imag-ined political community' of an emerging English (and nascent British) nation. The contribution made by the theatre to this generational project of writing the *nation* of England into being was unique, for the playhouse provided a vibrant forum and the English history play provided a popular means for Elizabethan audiences to participate in that imagined community and in the twin processes of *remembering* and *forgetting* on which a shared sense of national history crucially depends and that Shakespeare foregrounds so trenchantly in *Henry V*.

Shakespeare's dramatic writing on English history drew on and helped to create the avid public appetite for all forms of writing on England's past. His English chronicle plays comprise nearly a third of his known dramatic output, particularly if we include his possible collaboration on *Sir Thomas More* (*c.* 1592–5, revised *c.* 1603–4) and *Edward III* (*c.* 1592–3). In the first Folio's table of contents Shakespeare's plays are listed under one of three headings, 'Comedies', 'Histories' and 'Tragedies'. Of the ten plays grouped as Histories, all were written in the 1590s with the exception of *Henry VIII* (*All is True*), which dates to 1613. In choosing plays for inclusion as Histories the Folio's compilers were clearly guided by the 'Englishness' of the history treated in the plays they selected. The Histories are listed in the table of contents in chronological order by reign, commencing with *King John*, which begins soon after the king was crowned in 1199, and concluding with *Henry VIII*, which ends with the birth of Princess Elizabeth and anticipates the reign of James VI and I. The eight intervening plays span a tumultuous period in medieval English history from 1397 to 1485. The Folio's chronological listing has sponsored a modern performance tradition in which these eight plays are performed as a historical cycle that begins with the deposition and murder of Richard II and concludes with

the death of Richard III and the accession of the first
Tudor monarch, Henry VII, who brought the civil wars
to an end by uniting the Yorkists and the Lancastrians
through marriage. In their preoccupation with political
violence Shakespeare's English histories show 'the very
age and body of the time his form and pressure' (*Hamlet*,
III.2.23–4). Civil war, factionalism and political assassi-
nation had made the Low Countries and France vulner-
able to Spanish domination; all three, and the bane of
civil war in particular, feature prominently in
Shakespeare's Histories – except for *Henry V*.

In place of civil war, *Henry V* presents a war of invasion led by a king of England in which a numerically
greatly superior opponent suffers a humiliating defeat at
the hands of a 'beggared host' (IV.2.41). In what would
prove the last English history he wrote during Elizabeth's
reign (1558–1603) Shakespeare reminded contemporary
audiences of a time when their ancestors emerged victo-
rious from a battle undertaken against seeming impos-
sible odds and forced their enemies to sue for peace. The
posture of readiness, long endured by the English in their
defensive wars with Spain, is displaced on to the French,
who are reminded by the Dauphin 'that defences, musters,
preparations, | Should be maintained, assembled, and
collected, | As were a war in expectation' (II.4.18–20).
Where the preceding histories portray England divided
against itself, in *Henry V* Shakespeare creates the illusion
of a kingdom uniquely united in war against a foreign
adversary by omitting the anti-Lancastrian and dissenting
Lollard revolts Henry V had had to quell in the first
eighteen months of his reign, isolating the Cambridge
conspiracy as the only internal challenge to Henry's
regime and suppressing its political motive to depose
Henry in favour of Edmund Mortimer, Richard II's lineal

heir. He also makes the King of France a more regal opponent by omitting his name and any mention of the 'old disease of frensie' from which Charles VI reportedly suffered (Holinshed, _Chronicles_, vol. 3, p. 547). Far from being a distracted ruler troubled by bouts of mental illness, in _Henry V_ the King of France is the first to apprehend the gravity of the threat posed by Henry (II.4.48–9). The first two acts are given over to the preparations for war while the remaining three depict a radically foreshortened version of Henry V's French wars, portraying events from his first invasion of France in 1414 to the battle of Agincourt in 1415 before proceeding directly to Henry's betrothal to Princess Katherine, which sealed the peace treaty signed at Troyes cathedral in 1420. The intervening four-year period of sustained fighting is omitted, as is Henry's second French campaign, which was triggered by the Dauphin's rejection of the Treaty of Troyes and ended with Henry's death in 1422, probably from dysentery. This structure gives the play a double climax in the form of Henry's decisive victory at Agincourt and his betrothal to Katherine, war and peace, followed by the abrupt anticlimax of the Epilogue. Shakespeare would return to his abiding preoccupation with civil war in his next play, _Julius Caesar_, seen by a Swiss visitor at the Globe Theatre on 21 September 1599, one week before Essex's unauthorized return from Ireland. (The reference in the fifth chorus of _Henry V_ to the senators and plebeians of 'th'antique Rome' fetching in 'their conquering Caesar' (26–8) and the playwright's first ever mention of Mark Antony (III.6.14) together suggest that Shakespeare was already casting his mind forward to _Julius Caesar_ as he was completing _Henry V_.) In the years to follow Shakespeare would draw on Roman history for _Antony and Cleopatra_ and _Coriolanus_, on ancient

British legend for *King Lear* and *Cymbeline* and on Scottish history for *Macbeth*; however, it would be another fourteen years before he returned to the recent English past to write one of his last plays, *Henry VIII (All is True)*, probably in collaboration with John Fletcher. *Henry V* thus marks an important transition in the playwright's use of history on the stage.

The last of Shakespeare's Elizabethan chronicle histories, *Henry V* is also the last of a series of four plays known as the second tetralogy, so called because the plays that comprise the series (*Richard II, Henry IV, Parts I and II* and *Henry V*) were written after an earlier quartet of plays on the reigns of Henry VI and Richard III known as the first tetralogy. Although composed *after* the first tetralogy, the second tetralogy surveys the tumultuous twenty-three-year period in medieval English history (1397–1420) that immediately *preceded* the protracted wars over the royal succession portrayed in the earlier tetralogy. The events leading up to and following immediately upon the deposition and murder of Richard II are the subject of the first play in the second tetralogy. The next two plays, *Henry IV, Parts I and II*, treat the 'scambling and unquiet' (I.1.4) reign of Richard's successor, the usurper Henry Bolingbroke, who was the father of Prince Hal, the future King Henry V. *Henry V* brings the second tetralogy to a close, but its Epilogue recollects what came after: the premature death of Henry V and the coronation of his infant son Henry VI, 'Whose state so many had the managing | That they lost France, and made his England bleed' (11–12) – a history, it reminds audiences, 'Which oft our stage hath shown' (13). The chronological listing of Shakespeare's Histories in the first Folio thus suppresses one of the defining features of his double cycle of English history plays; namely, that it circles back on itself. The Epilogue to *Henry V* anticipates the death of Henry V, whose solemn funeral procession begins *Henry VI, Part I*. To the extent that the order of composition discloses the order of the writer's imagination, the reign of Henry V emerges as central and his untimely death as structurally and conceptually pivotal to a nostalgic project of recovery in which chronological order is subordinate to the order of remembrance, the linear narrative of time transformed by Shakespeare into a dramatic narrative that encircles irrecoverable loss. *Henry V* is the capstone of that narrative, the play that revives a fleeting vision of England's heroic past and 'Awake[ns] remembrance of [its] valiant dead' (I.2.115).

THE SPECTRE OF HENRY V

Henry V holds a unique place in Shakespeare's historical imagination, but Shakespeare was by no means the only Elizabethan playwright to detect in Henry V's short reign material likely to excite the interest of wartime audiences. By the time a version of Shakespeare's *Henry V* was performed in London playgoers had already had the opportunity to see as many as three other plays about England's conqueror-king since the mid 1580s. The most popular, and the one that had the greatest influence on Shakespeare's *Henry V* and *Henry IV* plays, was *The Famous Victories of Henry the fifth: Containing the Honourable Battell of Agin-court*, an anonymously written work printed by Thomas Creede in 1598. *Famous Victories* may have been performed by the Queen's Men as early as 1588, when anticipation of the threatened Spanish Armada was at its height. The text betrays nothing of the panic that reports of an approaching armada generated in

the capital just over a decade later. A bellicose play for a
bellicose time, *Famous Victories* reflects a national mood
of defiance, confidently alternating scenes of clowning
with scenes of conquest that pander unabashedly to
jingoist and chauvinist sentiments: if the King of France
does not consent to give his daughter in marriage to Henry,
Henry will 'so rouse the towers over his ears | That I
would make him be glad to bring her me | Upon his hands
and knees' (sc. xviii, ll. 71–3). The French soldiers (though
not the French king) are boastful or stupid; the innova-
tive tactics used by the English to secure victory are twice
noted; King Henry exhibits no sign of a conscience (troubled or otherwise) before battle; a bluff warrior, he proves
a brisk wooer – 'Ay but I love her, and must crave her –
| Nay, I love her, and will have her!' (sc. xviii, ll. 35–6);
for her part, having gained her father's consent, the French
princess is eager to be wed – 'I had best whilst he is willing,
| Lest when I would he will not' (sc. xx, ll. 48–9).

The appeal these earlier Henry V plays held for
Elizabethan audiences living amid the rumours and
reports of war can be gleaned from a passage in Nashe's
Pierce Penniless (1592) in which he observes 'what a
glorious thing it is to have Henry the fifth represented
on the stage, leading the French king prisoner, and forcing
both him and the Dauphin to swear fealty' (*Works*, vol.
I, p. 213). *Famous Victories* ends with a similar spectacle
of French humiliation in which Burgundy and the
Dolphin (probably a deliberate misspelling) are made to
swear fealty and kiss Henry's sword (sc. xx, ll. 34, 35), a
crowd-pleasing piece of stage business that Shakespeare
notably omits by having *Henry V* conclude just after
Henry demands oaths of submission from the French
peers but before they are performed (V.2.362–6). For
audiences living under renewed threat of invasion and

subject to alarmist reports of Spanish landings in Devon, Cornwall, Wales, Ireland and on the Isle of Wight, the appeal of Henry V and his against-the-odds victory at Agincourt is obvious.

In Shakespeare's English history plays the reign of Henry V similarly occasions a mixture of eager antici- pation and nostalgic longing. His *Henry VI* plays are haunted by the spectre of Henry V, whose reign becomes the focus of intense yearning for a former, idealized age of heroic conquests abroad and unity at home. Speakers in these plays repeatedly summon up remembrance of Henry V and his triumphs over the French. Even the ardent French patriot Joan la Pucelle (Joan of Arc), self- proclaimed scourge of the English, acknowledges the glory he achieved through his victories in France. Yet 'Glory', she observes, 'is like a circle in the water, | Which never ceaseth to enlarge itself | Till by broad spreading it disperse to naught' (*Henry VI, Part I*, I.2.133–5). So it is with Henry V, the foremost exemplar of English martial glory: 'With Henry's death the English circle ends; | Dispersèd are the glories it included' (136–7).

Tellingly, it is not Henry's life but his death that links the two tetralogies, where it serves as a poignant reminder of former glory. *Henry VI, Part I* begins with the funeral procession of Henry V, whose eulogy is laden with fore- boding:

> Posterity, await for wretched years,
> When at their mothers' moistened eyes babes shall suck,
> Our isle be made a nourish of salt tears,
> And none but women left to wail the dead. (I.1.48–51)

The premature death of its conquering hero has left England feminized and infantilized. His passing signals the demise of a masculine heroic ideal – 'arms avail not, now that Henry's dead' (47). The military victories Henry V achieved in France are the benchmark against which succeeding kings are measured and found wanting, such is the conviction that 'England ne'er lost a king of so much worth' (7). The reign of Henry VI sees the loss of his father's conquests and the advent of civil war, accentuating the desire for a return to an idealized past epitomized by the reign of the deceased king. Paradoxically, rather than securing the throne for his son, the glory achieved by Henry V ends up fuelling the sedition that deprives his son of both crown and life, because Henry VI's opponents are able to cite his squandering of his father's legacy as evidence of his unworthiness to rule.

In the plays of the second tetralogy the focus on Prince Hal, the future King Henry V, grows steadily more intense. The one play in which Henry V does not appear as either prince or king is _Richard II_, where his absence provokes his father to enquire 'Can no man tell me of my unthrifty son?' (V.3.1). Although _Henry IV, Parts I_ and _II_ are titled after the reigning king, Prince Hal appears in more scenes and speaks considerably more lines than does his ailing father. Yet Shakespeare's depiction of Hal as a politically knowing, role-playing heir to a tainted royal title significantly complicates the received legend of the prodigal prince. Although Hal's pledge at the outset of _Henry IV, Part I_ that he will 'so offend, to make offence a skill, | Redeeming time when men think least I will' (I.2.214–15) heightens the sense of anticipation that surrounds his long delayed accession to the throne at the end of _Henry IV, Part II_, it also frames his future 'sudden' reformation as a premeditated political stratagem devised by an astute tactician. The Prologue to _Henry V_ draws on the climate of expectation built up over the preceding seven plays; however, the ensuing depiction of Henry V and his French campaign is considerably more complex and disquieting than may have been anticipated of a ruler so long the object of nostalgic idealization. For the 'long' version of *Henry V* awakens remembrance of an English legend in such a way as to expose how such national legends are 'perfected', by reminding us of what we must forget to remember if they are to be sustained.

SHAKESPEARE'S THEATRE OF JUDGEMENT

The two figures in *Henry V* who are most determined to control how the past is remembered for political ends are Henry and his admiring Chorus. Yet even as the Chorus strives to fashion our thoughts, the dramatic sequence casts doubt on the choric version of events. In this artfully constructed drama the baffling inconsistencies between the choric commentary and the dramatic action play an essential part in promoting a theatre of judgement in the face of the strenuous efforts of the King and his Chorus to exploit eloquence to influence remembrance. Although the relentlessly flattering portrait of Henry V sketched in the choruses could hardly be more disambiguated, the Chorus frames the play with a pair of strikingly discordant speeches as Prologue and Epilogue and proves an unreliable narrator throughout. As regards the Prologue, it is hard to imagine a dramatic apostrophe more at odds with its theatrical occasion. Dramatic prologues and epilogues routinely seek the audience's pardon for supposed 'faults' in a play or performance, but few express as little confidence in the theatre as a mode of representation as does the Prologue to *Henry V*. For the prologue to a play about a famous royal martialist to apologize for the inadequacy of the 'crookèd figure' (15) of the actor and the 'wooden O' (13) of the theatre 'to bring forth | So great an object' (10–11) as the battle of Agincourt does not inspire confidence in playgoers recently parted from their money. Given the popular success of the *Henry VI* plays with their numerous battle scenes and bouts of sword fighting, the Prologue's poor opinion of the theatre's capacity to create credible martial spectacle appears perverse.

Although the Prologue disparages the shortcomings of theatrical spectacle, it expresses no such reservations about the capacity of speech to work on the listener's imagination or about the power of the imagination to 'Piece out . . . imperfections' (23) in the theatrical representation of Henry V and his French wars. On the contrary, the Chorus will exploit a heady combination of flattery, exhortation, hyperbole and 'invention' (2; the generation of material with which to move and convince) to persuade listeners 'Gently to *hear*, kindly to judge, our play' (34; added emphasis). While playbook prefaces were customarily addressed to 'Gentlemen Readers' (Erne, *Shakespeare as Literary Dramatist*, pp. 47–50), in the theatre the Prologue's 'gentles all' (8) flatters the many playgoers ranked beneath the gentry. Though subsequent choruses are more strident, this early posture of extreme obsequiousness and apologetic deference is never entirely abandoned. Exhorting us one moment, cajoling and imploring us the next, the strain required to convince us that we are witnessing a heroic epic becomes palpable. In the absence of 'A kingdom for a stage, princes to act, | And monarchs to behold the swelling scene' (3–4), the Prologue resorts to verbal amplification to overcome the physical limitations of the stage. With its rhetoric of 'a thousand parts' (24), it is the first in a series of choric speeches redolent of the abundant style. If the Prologue is to be believed, hyperbole must substitute for theatrical illusion because it alone has the power to foster the impression of plenitude and amplitude needed to induce us to 'make imaginary puissance' (25) and *see* 'warlike Harry ... Assume the port of Mars' (5–6) in our minds. The impression of heroic greatness is dependent on rhetorical invention and amplification, effective spectacle on affective speech.

'Think, when we talk ... you see' (Prologue.26) is the formula that informs the choruses. At key moments the Chorus invites us to imagine scenes of splendour the play makes no attempt to stage: 'The well-appointed King at Hampton pier ... and his brave fleet' (III.Chorus.4–5); 'The Mayor and all his brethren ... With the plebeians swarming at their heels', pouring out of London to 'fetch their conquering Caesar in' (V.Chorus.25–8). These lengthy passages of description draw needless attention to the limits of Elizabethan staging. The declared aim of the Chorus is to encourage us to tolerate 'th'excuse | Of time, of numbers, and due course of things' (V.Chorus. 3–4) in the performance, yet as Shakespeare nowhere else deemed the practice of abridgement he routinely adopted in composing history plays merited comment, much less an apology (44), the stated motives of the Chorus are suspect. The true purpose of these evocative speeches is not to inform us but to arouse our emotions and shape our thoughts. For it is by conjuring up a stirring vision of epic grandeur in our minds, a vision expressly *not* depicted on stage, that the Chorus entices us to accept its version of history as true in defiance of the evidence of our own eyes. As the stage direction calling for the entrance of '*the King and his poor soldiers*' (III.6.84), the

Constable's dismissive appraisal of Henry's army as a 'poor and starvèd band' (IV.2.14) and Henry's frank admission 'We are but warriors for the working-day' (IV.3.109) make plain, what we should witness is an altogether grimmer, more prosaic struggle, if one no less moving for its potent mix of humour and horror.

'Still be kind,' entreats the solicitous Chorus, 'And eke out our performance with your mind' (III.Chorus.34–5). In _The Winter's Tale_ Paulina instructs Leontes that if he wishes to see the statue of his wronged wife move and speak to him 'It is required | You do awake your faith' (V.3.94–5). Moments later Hermione '_slowly descends_' from her plinth (V.3.103). Keeping faith with the Chorus in _Henry V_ brings no such tangible reward for audiences, as what we see (directors permitting) doesn't merely fall short of the Chorus's vivid verbal scene-painting; on a number of occasions the ensuing action is blatantly at odds with the choric account, not least because the Chorus fails to acknowledge the existence of the Eastcheapers. The second chorus, for example, courteously announces that 'the scene | Is now transported, gentles, to Southampton' (34–5). Despite reiterating the shift in locale (41–2), what follows is not the anticipated sight of English youth, 'on fire' (1) with expectation, hurriedly preparing to embark from Southampton but a pub fight in Eastcheap between two of Falstaff's drinking companions over a brothel keeper and an unpaid debt. The Chorus's claim that 'honour's thought | Reigns solely in the breast of every man' (3–4) is similarly contradicted not only by the treachery of the three conspirators, whose existence the Chorus does acknowledge (21–30), but also by Pistol's cynical decision to join Henry's army as a supplier of provisions in anticipation that 'profits will accrue' (II.1.107). Later, rather than seeing an army of 'culled and choice-drawn cavaliers', supported by 'the nimble gunner', sweeping its way to victory at Harfleur as promised by the Act III Chorus (24, 32), we witness an army debilitated by sickness (III.3.55–6) undertake a second unsuccessful assault on the town's walls, during which a reluctant crew of Eastcheapers have to be beaten forward by Fluellen (III.2.20–1). Contrary to what the Act IV Chorus affirms, we do not see the English king on the eve of Agincourt 'Walking from watch to watch, from tent to tent . . . With cheerful semblance, and sweet majesty', dispensing to all 'A little touch of Harry in the night' (28–47). It may be that here, as elsewhere, the Chorus is relating an episode that has already occurred, yet when he has the opportunity to offer a group of sleepless soldiers words of encouragement we witness Henry do the very opposite by reporting that a trusted commander believes they are 'Even as men wrecked upon a sand, that look to be washed off the next tide' (IV.1.95–6), then heatedly quarrelling with them. These marked discrepancies between the choric report and the dramatic sequence draw attention to the gulf between the idealized account and the unembellished event.

Of the many discontinuities between the choric narrative and the ensuing action, none is more jarring or more salutary than that created by the abrupt transition from the Prologue to the opening scene. Working on our 'imaginary forces', the Prologue invites us to 'Suppose' that we see the combined forces of France and England crammed within the confines of the theatre (18–20). Moments later there step on to the stage not 'two mighty monarchies' (20), as we had been led to anticipate, but two scheming clerics calculating how best to block or moderate a bill, presently being re-urged in Parliament, that would divest the Church of 'the better half' (I.1.8)

of its landed wealth and use some of the funds to relieve
the poor, the sick and the elderly (15–17). This highly
equivocal scene provides an important template for the
play. Because the bill must receive royal assent before it
can become law, determining whether or not Henry can
be induced to oppose the measure is crucial to the two
bishops. It is in this context that Canterbury recounts
'The noble change' (*Henry IV, Part II*, IV.5.155) from
'wildness' to sobriety that Henry appeared to undergo
the moment his father died. Canterbury appears to offer
an adulatory account of Henry's spiritual reformation:

> Never was such a sudden scholar made;
> Never came reformation in a flood
> With such a heady currance scouring faults;
> Nor never Hydra-headed wilfulness
> So soon did lose his seat, and all at once,
> As in this King. (I.1.32–7)

Yet, by underscoring the singularity of the sudden and
improbable change from 'Hydra-headed wilfulness' to 'a
paradise | T'envelop and contain celestial spirits' (I.1.30–
31), his thrice repeated 'never' can also sound incredu-
lous. The archbishop has difficulty explaining how a
seemingly dissolute prince, who never appeared to devote
any time to private study, came to possess the skills of
an accomplished statesman. Henry's 'discourse of war'
(43) may be accounted for by his having experienced
combat during his father's troubled reign, but as he point-
edly distanced himself from his father's court, preferring
the companionship of the Boar's Head tavern to affairs
of state, his ability to address matters of policy and reli-
gion with seeming ease and fluency on becoming king is
no less wondrous than his sudden reformation. As

Canterbury observes, it 'is a wonder how his grace should glean it, | Since his addiction was to courses vain, | His companies unlettered, rude, and shallow' (I.1.53–5).

The key to the riddle of Henry's duplex reformation is supplied by Canterbury in his second panegyric. If we listen closely as each of Henry's virtues is listed, his defining skill as a ruler becomes apparent:

> *Hear* him but reason in divinity,
> And all-admiring, with *an inward wish*,
> You would desire the King were made a prelate.
> *Hear* him *debate* of commonwealth affairs,
> You would say it hath been all in all his study.
> *List* his *discourse* of war, and you shall *hear*
> A fearful battle rendered you *in music*.
> Turn him to any cause of policy,
> The Gordian knot of it he will unloose,
> Familiar as his garter; that, when he *speaks*,
> The air, a chartered libertine, is still,
> And the *mute wonder lurketh in men's ears*
> To steal his *sweet and honeyed sentences*.
>   (I.1.38–50; added emphasis)

Every instance Canterbury cites of Henry's proficiency as a ruler is rooted in Henry's virtuosity as a public speaker. Such is the seductive power of the king's copious, captivating, almost cloying speech that he doesn't just sound the part, according to the archbishop Henry's eloquence so enchants his listeners that 'with an inward wish' they desire him to be the person his speech enables him successively to resemble. Significantly, the response Henry's oratory solicits is not dialogue or debate but 'mute wonder'. A pattern of Henry using exceedingly protracted speeches to silence dissent is readily detectable in the play: the Southampton conspirators say little in their own defence after Henry's prolonged tirade; the Governor of Harfleur surrenders the town immediately after Henry's sustained threatening speech; and Katherine, having hardly spoken as Henry displays at length his mastery of the plain style favoured by Hotspur in *Henry IV, Part I*, falls silent after Henry's forced kiss. Revealingly, when Henry's disguise obliges him to debate with his soldiers on equal terms (IV.1.90–222) he ends up engaged in a bitter quarrel over ethics that climaxes in an intemperate exchange of gages. Willing obedience is the aim of the orator king, as it is of his tireless accomplice in persuasion the Chorus, and Williams's blunt reminder that subjects are constrained to obey angers this self-styled 'king of good fellows' (V.2.240).

Canterbury's damaging disclosure that he has already discussed matters 'touching France' with the king and pledged 'to give a greater sum' to fund Henry's wars than the clergy had given to any of his predecessors (I.1.75–81) means that when Henry publicly charges this scheming cleric to 'justly and religiously unfold' (I.2.10) whether or not the Salic law bars him from claiming the French crown, he knows full well (as do we) that the archbishop will support his claim and has a financial motive for doing so. This revelation compounds those niggling doubts and insinuations that unsettle Canterbury's apparently laudatory portrait of the king and detracts from Henry's heroic image even as it is being constructed and seemingly venerated. This corrosive quality is not unique to Canterbury; paradoxically, the unreliable choruses ensure it is integral to the play's design. Incorporating such verbal slippages and dramatic discontinuities at the outset attunes our ears to dissonance and our eyes to dissimulation. By the end of their exchange Canterbury, who initially appeared to subscribe, however knowingly, to the legend of Hal's miraculous reformation, concurs with Ely that the transformation of the profligate prince into the reformed king was premeditated:

> It must be so, for miracles are ceased;
> And therefore we must needs admit the means
> How things are perfected. (I.1.67–9)

The statement 'we must needs admit the means | How things are perfected' is an apt gloss on *Henry V*. While the apparently fulsome praise Henry receives from the two clergymen invites us to embrace the legend of his reformation unthinkingly, the stark disparity between the appearance of piety and the crass shoring-up of riches in the opening scene, like that between the Prologue's invocation of 'a Muse of fire' (1) and the cynical voices that succeed it, encourages us to reflect critically on the historical legend and to exercise judgement in responding to the play. Above all the opening exchange between these two wily bishops cautions us to be wary of the Chorus's stirring invocations of an imperial pageant by directing attention to how such sanitized accounts of royal power are constructed and the political ends they serve. 'Yet sit and see,' the Chorus urges, 'Minding true things by what their mockeries be' (IV.Chorus.52–3). So numerous, manifest and consistent are the discrepancies between the Chorus's pronouncements and the ensuing action that the idealized choric account is gradually exposed as a distortion of 'true things' – so long, that is, as audiences and directors resist the Chorus's urgent solicitations, remember the sequence of events and respond judiciously to beguiling oratory, 'Not working with the eye without the ear, | And but in purgèd judgement trusting neither' (II.2.135–6).

Fluellen provides an object lesson in the hazards of failing to measure words against deeds when he mistakes Pistol to be courageous. The Boy has already confided that 'Pistol . . . hath a killing tongue, and a quiet sword' (III.2.34), yet Fluellen claims that he witnessed an unnamed ensign, subsequently revealed to be Pistol, 'do . . . gallant service' defending the bridge (III.6.12–15). Only later do we discover that Fluellen's high regard for Pistol did not in fact arise from the *sight* of Pistol's 'gallant service' but from the *sound* of his 'prave words' at such bridge. Fluellen's comical confusion of sound with sight in his muddled simile, "a uttered as prave words at the pridge as you shall see in a summer's day' (III.6.62–3), exemplifies his tendency to mistake words for deeds. In advising his fellow captain, 'you must learn to know such slanders of the age' (III.6.78–9), Gower recalls the words of Ely in the opening scene and reaffirms the play's preoccupation with the power of speech to shape perceptions of the truth.

Our ability to distinguish between seeming and substance (and to remember the sequence of events) is similarly tested, and not just by the choruses. The greatest tests of our judgement follow the battle of Agincourt. After hearing the disproportionate losses suffered by the French Henry attributes his victory entirely to God: 'O God, Thy arm was here! | And not to us, but to Thy arm alone, | Ascribe we all!' (IV.8.105–7). By omitting any mention of the tactics employed to defeat the French, Shakespeare allows Henry's claim that divine intervention alone could account for such a resounding upset to appear more credible. The one notable exception is the playwright's retention of Henry's command to kill the French prisoners (IV.6.37). Yet many may be lured by Gower's misconstruing of events (IV.7.5–10) into believing that the order is given after the king learns that the boys have been killed when in fact Shakespeare departs from the chronicles of Hall and Holinshed in making Henry's order precede the raid on the English camp, radically altering its motivation.

An earlier scene provides weightier grounds for questioning whether Henry's account of the battle is any more accurate than Gower's by exposing another, far-reaching cause for the stunning collapse of the French army at Agincourt. Whether we do so depends yet again on our willingness to exercise our faculties of memory and judgement. After their initial boisterous assault on the English has been repulsed Orleans observes to Bourbon and the Constable that the scattered French forces would still be of sufficient number to overwhelm their opponents 'If any order might be thought upon' (IV.5.21). When Henry hears a fresh alarm sounded in the field he promptly commands his soldiers to execute their prisoners in the mistaken belief that just such a regrouping is underway (IV.6.35–8). Fatally, the French nobles refuse to observe any such collective discipline. The responses of Bourbon and the Constable – 'The devil take order', 'Disorder that hath spoiled us, friend us now! | Let us on heaps go offer up our lives' (IV.5.22, 17–18) – clarify both why their first impetuous and over-confident attack failed and why the French nobility are slaughtered in such numbers. Formerly the subject of lewdly convivial banter, in battle their adherence to a medieval chivalric code founded on individual feats of valour against opponents of noble blood impels even the most level-headed among them to bury shame in death once they believe that their honour has been sullied irredeemably by their initial, shameful repulse at the hands of Henry's 'beggared host' (IV.2.41). Sent to the field 'with spirit of honour edged, | More sharper than [their] swords' (III.5.38–9), their devotion to an aristocratic code of chivalric honour costs them the battle and many of them and their untitled foot soldiers their lives. As the staggeringly disproportionate casualty lists graphically testify, such a single-minded pursuit of personal repute is perilously outdated in a war in which the chivalric ideal of fellowship in arms is evoked by Exeter's report of the deaths of Suffolk and York (IV.6.7–27) only to be brutally displaced by Henry's merciless order to execute defenceless prisoners. In *Henry IV, Part I* the death of Hotspur is felt as a present loss; in *Henry V* the sentimental deaths of Suffolk and York occur as if in another, older world. Agincourt bears out Exeter's blunt warning to the King of France that Henry is prepared to abandon his posture as 'the native and true challenger' in a chivalric trial-by-combat and enforce his will through 'Bloody constraint' (III.2.71; cf. 79, 93–4). Unlike the French, the military discipline Henry imposes is strategic, collective and ruthless, as Bardolph, Nym and the French prisoners discover to their cost. The bookish concern with 'the Roman disciplines' (III.2.71; cf. 79, 93–4) that preoccupies Fluellen finds no echo in his king, who prudently consults the chronicles before declaring war on France merely to ascertain what other hazards may arise from such a decision and how best to counter them (I.2.146–54). Where the French commanders are preoccupied with their status and repute – a preoccupation Henry avowedly shares (I.2.226–34; IV.3.28–9) – as a military leader he imposes strict discipline on his army and ensures that it is ordered by military rank, each rank having its particular martial function. Such is Henry's confidence that his officers know their offices that his terse order before battle is framed as a statement of fact: 'You know your places' (IV.3.78).

In his Crispin Crispian oration (IV.3.18–67) Henry seeks
to rally the daunted spirits of his followers by appealing
to their shared desire to be remembered 'with advantages'
(50). The King is as acutely aware as the Chorus that how
history is remembered depends on whose history is told
and who does the telling. Of the many kings that appear
in Shakespeare's English histories, none is more anxious
than Henry V to control *which* story of his reign the 'good
man' shall 'teach his son' (56). His title as King of England
tainted by his father's deposition of Richard II and
Richard's subsequent murder, Henry V has every reason
to be concerned how his history is reported. The perceived
legitimacy and consequent stability of his reign and of the
Lancastrian dynasty are critically dependent on whether
he can achieve sufficient popular renown as a conquering
hero to expunge his father's crime from the collective
memory of his subjects and allay the threat of civil war
over the disputed succession by securing their devoted
loyalty. As we have seen, Shakespeare's early history plays
are haunted by the spectre of Henry V; on the night before
Agincourt we discover that Henry V is haunted by his
father's act of treason: 'Not today, O Lord, | O not today,
think not upon the fault | My father made in compassing
the crown!' (IV.1.285–7). Fearful that God may avenge his
father's crime in the coming battle, Henry anxiously
recounts the measures he has taken to expiate his father's
guilt and appease the soul of the murdered Richard. Henry
falsely claims that his acts of contrition are 'nothing worth'
because his 'penitence comes after all, | Imploring pardon'
(296–8); however, penitence always comes after the act
that is repented. The reason that Henry's public contrition
is hollow is that he is willing to speed Richard's soul to
heaven but unwilling to relinquish the English crown to
Richard's heirs.

'Piece out our imperfections with your thoughts ...'
the Prologue instructs the audience, 'For 'tis your
thoughts that now must deck our kings' (23–8). In his
soliloquy Henry disavows the doctrine of sacred kingship expounded by Richard II (*Richard II*, III.2.54–7,
193–201). Haunted by his father's crime and by the spectre
of political illegitimacy, he reflects on the theatricality of
monarchical authority. In a remarkable passage Henry
acknowledges that it is ceremony that empowers kings
by instilling the custom of obedience in their subjects,
'place, degree, and form, | Creating awe and fear in other
men' (IV.1.239–40). Yet that 'idol ceremony' (233), that
'proud dream' (250) inspiring belief becomes substantial.
The royal sceptre may be a mere stage property in political dramas played out on the scale of nations, but its
possessor can exact real tears and blood. So long as his
orders are obeyed, the king retains the power to end breath
with a breath: 'Then every soldier kill his prisoners! |
Give the *word* through' (IV.6.37–8; added emphasis).
Henry is fully conscious of the 'Twin-born' (IV.1.227)
nature of his authority: his dependence on popularity and
his consequent need to project greatness to secure his
subjects' loyalty and willing obedience.

As the son of a successful rebel, Henry V also knows
too well the deadly cost to any occupant of the throne
if responsibility and hence blame is heaped 'Upon the
King' (IV.1.223). Over the course of the play he is at
pains to disclaim his sovereign will. He transfers to the
irreligious Canterbury the burden of responsibility for
legitimizing his claim to France and sanctioning war
(I.2.9–32). The Dauphin's mocking gift of tennis balls is
blamed for causing the onset of hostilities and 'his soul',
not Henry's, 'Shall stand sore chargèd for the wasteful
vengeance | That shall fly with them' (I.2.282–9). The

suggestion that inanimate objects possess greater volition than a king is nonsense, though the fervency with which Henry delivers his 'merry message' (299) to the French ambassadors may mask its strained logic in performance. Henry's denial of mercy to the Southampton conspirators is their own fault: 'The mercy that was quick in us but late | By your own counsel is suppressed and killed' (II.2.79–80). Yet unlike the chronicles, which record that Henry immediately apprehended and sentenced the conspirators on learning of their plot, Shakespeare has Henry delay their public exposure and arrest precisely to ensure that, by first luring them into counselling against lenity in the case of the drunkard, he is relieved of blame for the severity of their punishment. Should he refuse to deliver up his crown to Henry, the King of France will be liable for

> ... the widows' tears, the orphans' cries,
> The dead men's blood, the privèd maidens' groans,
> For husbands, fathers, and betrothèd lovers
> That shall be swallowed in this controversy. (II.4.106–9)

As for the citizens of Harfleur, they too are 'guilty in defence' (III.3.43), and the disproportionate number of casualties suffered by the French at Agincourt is ascribed entirely to God (IV.8.105–11). Contrary to the Tudor chronicles, in which kings are represented as second only to God as the agents of historical events, Henry is singularly anxious to deny he plays a vital part in determining the chronological sequence of cause and effect. He sets about redeeming his tainted title by seeming to let be, presenting himself as the selfless agent of a providential ordering of time. In deposing Richard II, his father also deposed the doctrine of sacred kingship. Henry V in turn disclaims his sovereign power so that he can appear to be the chosen agent of divine providence, his blemished title redeemed not by the calculated assertion of his sovereign will or even by popular opinion but by the divine will of God. To accept his providential interpretation, however, we must forget to remember his inveterate role-playing, policy, military and self-discipline.

'WHAT ISH MY NATION?' (III.2.118)

Popularly celebrated as an English hero in Shakespeare's day, Henry V is an artificer of remembrance in Shakespeare's play. As for *Henry V*, it too seems at first glance a quintessentially 'English' history play that intervenes self-reflexively in the processes of remembering and forgetting on which notions of nation depend. And so it does, but in a much more unorthodox manner than might be anticipated given its subject. For among Shakespeare's English histories, *Henry V* is the most preoccupied with the matter of Britain. On the one hand, the words 'England' and 'English' occur more than one hundred times, ensuring that they resonate throughout the play (Schwyzer, *Literature, Nationalism and Memory*, p. 126). The leaders of the French forces repeatedly refer to their opponents as 'the English', and when he urges on his soldiers in battle Henry appeals to their Englishness, a trait he equates with manliness and martial ability. Yet, on the other, the emerging nation, whose former conquests in France under Henry V the Chorus seeks to fashion into a heroic patriotic epic, is elsewhere depicted as conspicuously hybrid, as are their French opponents. We have already noted how the 'strait strossers' of the Irish kern can be detected beneath the

'French hose' worn by Henry's opponents (III.7.51–2). For their part the French mockingly dismiss Henry's soldiers as 'Normans, but bastard Normans, Norman bastards!' (III.5.10), deriding their opponents as the illegitimate offspring of the Norman French who invaded and colonized England in the eleventh century. However, in disparaging their adversaries as ignoble bastards, 'the French-cum-Irish', as one commentator aptly describes them (Altman, '"Vile Participation"', p. 19), inadvertently foreshadow their own defeat at the hands of the invaders by assigning to their opponents the hybrid identity of the Anglo-Normans who invaded and colonized Ireland in the twelfth century. Though he mocks 'the English' as a mongrel people, the Dauphin confesses that

> Our madams mock at us, and plainly say
> Our mettle is bred out, and they will give
> Their bodies to the lust of English youth,
> To new-store France with bastard warriors. (III.5.28–31)

Over-cultivation depletes virility necessitating an injection of 'wild and savage stock' (7) to restore vigour. In a further complication, the prevalent French conception of the English as 'a barbarous people' (4) who nonetheless display extraordinary daring in battle (15–20) closely echoes prevailing English perceptions of the 'wild Irish'. 'Irishness' thus figures in the play as a trait that is both native and alien, immanent and elusive, to be feared for its savagery and admired for its hardiness even as it is mocked.

Meanwhile the outline of a composite British identity, based for the most part on an amalgamation of national stereotypes, is generated by Shakespeare's introduction of a quartet of captains who between them represent the

four 'nations' that make up the British isles. Although
other characters refer to them by name, the speech-
prefixes '*Welch.*', '*Scot.*' and '*Irish.*' used in the first Folio
reduce Fluellen, Jamy and Macmorris to their respective
national identities, while their speeches and verbal tics
further reduce all three to national stereotypes for comic
effect (a treatment from which Gower is uniquely
exempt). For a fleeting moment the joint entrance of the
Scottish and Irish captains appears to confirm contemporary English concerns over Scottish collusion in
Ireland, only for Jamy's determination to do 'gud service'
(III.2.111) immediately to allay such anxieties. With their
discordant voices and disparate mindsets, the interactions
among the four captains resemble the workings of
Canterbury's beehive whereby 'many things, having full
reference | To one consent, may work contrariously,
[yet] . . . End in one purpose' (I.2.205–13). What they
singularly fail to generate is an image of a harmoniously
united British 'nation', though their quarrelling and
mutual rivalry does put comic pay to residual English
fears of a hostile 'pan-Celtic' military alliance (Highley,
Shakespeare, Spenser and the Crisis in Ireland, p. 146). In
place of the threatening spectre of encirclement, the play
offers English audiences an alluring fantasy of assimilation in which neighbouring Celtic nations willingly
become subsumed within the English (nascent British)
imperial effort. The violent imposition of English rule is
tactfully displaced from the British isles to France, and
resistant Celts mutate into enthusiastic collaborators
in the conquest of a neighbouring nation by a king of
England.

The use of the Anglicized form of the Welsh name
'Lluellen' suggests that Fluellen is the most assimilated
of the Celtic captains, until we reflect that the surname

of the fully assimilated 'English' captain, Gower, carries both English and Welsh associations. For English audience members, the readiest link is to the Yorkshire poet John Gower, a contemporary of Geoffrey Chaucer. John Gower appears in *Pericles* (*c.* 1607), which derives its story from Book 8 of Gower's poem *Confessio Amantis* (1390). For Welsh playgoers, Gower is a name associated with the ancient Marcher lordship of Gower in south Wales (Lloyd, *Speak It in Welsh*, pp. 72–3). After its colonization by English speakers, the lordship was divided into English and Welsh Gower, a linguistic division between the southern and northern portions of the region that survives to the present day. The 'English' captain can therefore also be viewed as a fully assimilated Welshman, as can Williams. Williams's speech, like Gower's, is unmarked by putative Welsh traits, yet Williams, like Fluellen, bears an Anglicized version of a (common) Welsh surname, an English 's' substituting for the Welsh prefix '*ap*' ('son of').

The periodic alternation of Fluellen's speech-prefix between '*Flu.*' and '*Welch.*', the former placing him on a par with the consistently individuated Captain Gower and the latter reducing him to a national stereotype on a par with the '*Scot.*' Jamy and the '*Irish.*' Macmorris, reflects the medial position Wales occupied at the close of the sixteenth century as the most politically absorbed of England's Celtic neighbours. Within the Lancastrian tetralogy Fluellen acts as the mirror opposite of Owen Glendower: where the 'irregular and wild Glendower' (*Henry IV, Part I*, I.1.40) leads a Welsh revolt against Henry IV in *Henry IV, Part I*, two plays and a succession later Fluellen is Henry V's most dedicated follower excepting the Chorus. So fervent is Fluellen's commitment to Henry's aggressively expansionist aims that it is he who beats the dawdling Eastcheapers forward to the breach at Harfleur, he who subjects Pistol to 'a Welsh correction' in order to teach the unruly Eastcheaper 'a good English condition' (V.1.74–5), and he who immodestly compares Henry of Monmouth to Alexander the Great (or 'Pig') of Macedon (IV.7.11–51). Fluellen's account of the origins of the leek as a Welsh emblem epitomizes his internalization of the English colonizer's values. Rather than being the symbol of an autonomous nation with a distinct culture, the leek becomes 'an honourable badge of the service' Welshmen performed for an English king at the battle of Crécy 'in a garden where leeks did grow' (IV.7.90–99). Fluellen's conception of Welshness as a trait exemplified in military service to the English crown would be reassuring to English audiences, especially at a time when the Welsh were proving particularly resistant to service in Elizabeth's wars in Ireland (Highley, p. 156).

However, the violent quarrel between Fluellen and Macmorris destabilizes the prospect of assimilation fostered by the presence of the four captains in Henry's army, as it exposes lingering rifts over ethnic and national identity within the embryonic British nation. For Macmorris the question of national identity remains deeply fraught and potentially explosive. When Fluellen appears to disparage his 'nation' for its lack of learning Macmorris abruptly interrupts before Fluellen can utter the familiar racist insults: 'Ish a villain, and a bastard, and a knave, and a rascal. What ish my nation? Who talks of my nation?' (III.2.118–20). But determining just which 'nation' Fluellen is on the point of impugning is problematic because Macmorris's national identity is difficult to stabilize. Although the speech-prefix used in the Folio identifies Macmorris (spelt 'Makmorrice' or

'Mackmorrice') as '*Irish.*', his patronymic (literally 'son of Maurice') conjoins the Gaelic Irish prefix 'Mac' to an Anglicized form of a Norman termination (cf. P. Barton quoted in Hopkins, 'Neighbourhood', p. 16). Distrust of the loyalty of all Irishmen was widespread among the English during the Nine Years War, regardless of whether they were Gaels (whom the English referred to dismissively as 'Macs') or descendants of the twelfth-century Anglo-Norman colonizers known as the Old English or Palesmen, as they suspected many of the latter had 'gone native' after centuries living alongside the 'wild Irish'. Macmorris's hybrid surname neatly encapsulates such fears. As a descendant of the Old English community in Ireland, a population regarded to be more English than Gaelic by the Gaels and more Gaelic than English by New English colonists (Maley, 'Shakespeare, Holinshed and Ireland', pp. 33–4; Highley, p. 145), Macmorris is simultaneously aligned with and excluded from both an Irish and an English national identity. It is therefore unsurprising that Macmorris's urgent question 'What ish my nation?' remains unanswered. Although Gower reputes Macmorris 'a very valiant gentleman' (III.2.64–5) and admonishes both captains that they 'mistake each other' (129), Macmorris's Gaelic-Anglo-Norman identity, cod-Irish accent and matter-of-fact approach to acts of extreme violence ensure that he remains an object of suspicion and savage otherness for English audiences. That is until Henry, having directed his soldiers to 'imitate the action of the tiger' (III.1.6), matches Macmorris's threat to decapitate Fluellen (III.2.128) with a promise to be 'a clipper' and 'cut French crowns' in battle (IV.1.220–22), orders his soldiers to kill their prisoners (IV.6.37) and speaks to Katherine 'plain soldier' (V.2.148–9). So riddled with reputed traits of Irishness is Henry's discourse of war that it is little wonder that Isabel greets the King of England with the anachronistic salutation 'brother Ireland' in the first Folio (see note to V.2.12).

In defiance of history, theatrical convention and audience expectations, the foremost exemplar of hybrid nationality in *Henry V* proves to be the selfsame 'royal Captain' (IV.Chorus.29) the second chorus extols as the model of English greatness (16). Although he Anglicizes his name to 'Harry', and the King of France and the Dauphin both refer to Henry V as 'our brother of England' (II.4.75, 115), 'Harry England' (III.5.48) or simply 'England' (II.4.9 and *passim*), on the two occasions when Henry assigns himself a national identity it is that of a Welshman. When Pistol mistakes 'Harry le Roy' for a Cornishman the disguised king firmly corrects him: 'No, I am a Welshman' (IV.1.49–51). Later Henry reassures Fluellen that he too wears a leek on Wales's national day of celebration, explaining 'For I am Welsh, you know' (IV.7.102–3). Fluellen's conviction that 'All the water in Wye cannot wash [the] Welsh plood' from Henry's body (IV.7.104–5) is characteristically effusive but genealogically unfounded, as although the historical Henry V was born at Monmouth in Wales and was the Prince of Wales before his accession to the English throne, he had no immediate Welsh ancestry (Schwyzer, p. 127). Shakespeare's transfusion of 'Welsh plood' into the English king's body flatters the Tudor dynasty by compounding Henry's identity with that of the Welshman Owain Tudur, who succeeded Henry V as the husband of Katherine and was an ancestor of Elizabeth I. As the Welsh claimed descent from the ancient Britons, Henry's avowals of his Welshness also play a vital role in enabling an English king to become the hero of an embryonic

British nation. Henry's wider purpose is to legitimize his kingly title and rule 'in large and ample empery' (I.2.227) by reviving England's imperial crown. In pursuit of that goal his Welshness, like his Irishness, remains firmly yoked to the harness of an expansive Englishness – 'Cry, "God for Harry, England, and Saint George!"' (III.1.34). In the process the boundaries of England are increasingly blurred, becoming at once more extensive and more permeable. When Rambures misconceives England as an island (III.7.137) he repeats the error of extending England's boundaries to make them coterminal with the island comprising England, Scotland and Wales previously committed by John of Gaunt in his 'sceptred isle' speech in *Richard II* (II.1).

At the close of the play Henry conjures up the vision of 'a boy, half French, half English, that shall go to Constantinople and take the Turk by the beard' (V.2.205–7). In a now familiar strategy of 'busy[ing] giddy minds | With foreign quarrels' (*Henry IV, Part II*, IV.5.213–14), Henry proposes to 'Plant neighbourhood and Christian-like accord' (V.2.345) between the divided kingdoms of France and England by exporting war to the margins of Europe and uniting the two Christian powers in a war against a common Muslim enemy that threatens Europe's borders and its extension eastward. Intermarriages patterned on his betrothal to Katherine are to be encouraged, 'That English may as French, French Englishmen, | Receive each other' (V.2.359–60). The elimination of division through the generation of hybrid national identities emerges not only as a corollary of war but also as the precondition of imperial expansion (Edwards, *Threshold of a Nation*, p. 71). Henry's ability to interpret Katherine's French and speak to her haltingly in her own language is consistent with his efforts over the preceding *Henry IV* plays to master his future subjects by mastering their verbal idioms. The Epilogue abruptly reminds us, however, that rather than expanding England's borders, enhancing its power and exporting war to the distant Turk, Henry's invasion of France and marriage to Katherine rapidly resulted in the very opposite. Instead of the indomitable warrior he envisaged as his heir, Henry was succeeded by a son 'in infant bands crowned King . . . Whose state so many had the managing | That they lost France, and made his England bleed' (Epilogue.9–12). Instead of dominating France, the French wife of Henry VI, Margaret of Anjou, would dominate the King of England and threaten the masculine heroic ideal espoused by Henry V and the Chorus by proving a more formidable warrior than her husband in the *Henry VI* plays, 'Which oft our stage hath shown' (13).

INVASION AND POSSESSION

Unlike the *Henry VI* plays to which the Epilogue alludes, where French women warriors such as Joan of Arc and Queen Margaret feature prominently, *Henry V* excludes women from appearing (or even being mentioned as appearing) on the battlefield, a feature that allies it with *Richard III* alone among Shakespeare's English histories (Howard and Rackin, *Engendering a Nation*, p. 198). The twin solicitations of the discourses of war in *Henry V* are to manliness and fraternity, gendered appeals that likewise exclude women. Faced with appalling odds at Agincourt, Henry invites his soldiers to join in fellowship with him and become a 'band of brothers' (IV.3.60) by sacrificing their blood in his cause. For its part, the third chorus portrays willing participation in Henry's campaign as a corollary of manliness. Only those males 'past or not arrived' at their adult strength and virility remain behind in England (21–4). When Henry urges his soldiers to renew their assault on Harfleur he depicts the attack as an opportunity to prove 'That those whom you called fathers did beget you' (III.1.23). Declaring war on France similarly affords Henry the opportunity to show that his forefathers' 'blood and courage' run in his veins (I.2.117–19). The legitimacy of both the king and his male subjects is affirmed by feats of martial courage, as if patrilineal succession did not depend on wives and mothers. Faced with a plethora of such gendered appeals and with only four female speaking roles, none comprising more than 2 per cent of the total lines, it is difficult not to conclude that *Henry V* banishes women to the margins of history. Pistol's parting instruction to his newly married wife Hostess Quickly, formerly sole owner of the Boar's Head tavern, 'Let housewifery appear. Keep close, I thee command' (II.3.58), is characteristic of a play in which none of the women ventures outside the enclosed space of either the tavern or the court, where their identities and duties are domesticated and their public roles curtailed. Although Isabel proposes to add 'a woman's voice' to the peace negotiations, they are not staged (V.2.92–4). Her public utterances conform to contemporary gender conventions where the woman's role is to secure the bonds between men. If women are marginalized as active agents of history and of nation-building in *Henry V*, their bodies nevertheless figure prominently in its discourses of invasion and possession. Set against this is the play's exposure of the limits of a martial ideal of manliness and Henry's reliance on female authority to uphold his right.

Held up as an English exemplar of the heroic masculine ideal by the Chorus, Henry's royal authority is nonetheless crucially dependent on Frenchwomen. Canterbury's commentary on the Salic law reminds audiences that the validity of Henry's claim to France relies on inheritance through the female line. The female in question, Queen Isabella, daughter of Philip IV of France and mother to Edward III of England, is never named, however, and the fact that Henry derives his title to the French crown from a French female is never broached again. When the archbishop invites Henry to 'Look back into your mighty ancestors' (I.2.102) the two 'valiant dead' (115) he nominates, Edward the Black Prince and Edward III, are both English and male. This alternative lineage of male English warriors swiftly supplants the French female from whom Henry's claim to France strictly derives. Thus when Exeter delivers Henry's message bidding the King of France to resign his crown he makes no mention of Isabella and instead declares that Henry bases his demand on his lineal descent 'From his most famed of famous ancestors, | Edward the Third' (II.4.91–5).

The King of France does not dispute Henry's lineal ties to Edward III and the Black Prince, nor does he doubt his power and resolve. However, his ready acceptance that Henry 'is a stem | Of that victorious stock' (62–3) is not entirely complimentary. Where the English celebrate Crécy as a famous victory, the King of France associates the battle with the haunting sight of Edward III, standing on a nearby mountain, smiling to see his son 'Mangle the work of nature, and deface | The patterns that by God and by French fathers | Had twenty years been made' (60–62). From the French perspective Henry's kinship with the Black Prince, who 'Forage[d] in blood of French nobility' (I.2.110), allies him with ungodly acts of bestial savagery. To admit that Henry is 'bred out of that bloody strain' (II.4.51) allows that there is cause to fear his 'native mightiness' (64), but it also implies dispraise of his potential barbarism.

The idealization of 'warlike Harry' and his military exploits in the choruses is further destabilized by the repeated association of war with sexual aggression towards women. Henry warns the citizens of Harfleur that continued resistance will result in the destruction of their families. The 'reverend heads' of their fathers will be 'dashed to the walls' (III.3.37) and their 'naked infants spitted upon pikes' (38), destroying the living bonds on which the transmission of patrilineality depends. Motivated by 'licentious wickedness' (22), 'th'enragèd soldiers in their spoil' (25) shall also expend their aggression on the town's 'fresh fair virgins' (14). The prospective violence targeted at the bodies of young women is presently sexualized by the English king:

> What is't to me, when you yourselves are cause,
> If your pure maidens fall into the hand
> Of hot and forcing violation?
> . . .
> Take pity of your town and of your people
> Whiles yet my soldiers are in my command,
> . . .
> If not, why, in a moment look to see
> The blind and bloody soldier with foul hand
> Defile the locks of your shrill-shrieking daughters . . .
> (19–35)

Raping young virgins is one of the spoils of war. Having selected the name of 'soldier' as the one 'that . . . becomes

me best' (5–6) – an identity he will reaffirm in his
courtship of Katherine – Henry is implicated in the figure
of the invader-as-rapist evoked in his speech. His subsequent instruction to Exeter to 'Use mercy to them all'
(54) distinguishes the king's conduct from that of a rapist.
Whether that order is sufficient to banish remembrance
of his earlier oration urging his soldiers to turn themselves into human battering rams (or erect phalluses)
with which to assault the breach in the walls of a feminized Harfleur (III.3.9) remains debatable, however.

The French peers too conceive of invasion as a form
of rape, which, if allowed to proceed unopposed, would
reduce them to the degrading status of a pimp who stood
'cap in hand' by the chamber-door as a lustful brute raped
his 'fairest daughter' (IV.5.12–16). Figuratively, and for
women also literally, armed invasion is synonymous with
the threat of sexual assault. As previously noted, in char-
acterizing their enemies as 'Norman bastards' Britaine
imputes that the English are the descendants of just such
a sexual 'contamination' of their foremothers by Norman
French invaders in the eleventh century. However, in an
important deviation from the rape motif, both he and the
Dauphin are concerned that Frenchwomen may willingly
'give | Their bodies to the lust of English youth'
(III.5.28–31), having adjudged their 'native lords' (26) to
be effeminate cowards. Put plainly, by penetrating the
country's borders and its women's bodies the invader
impugns the manliness and virility of its male inhabitants
whose duty it is to protect the nation's borders and 'their'
women's chastity inviolate.

The twin distinctions between forceful possession of
and dependence on women, compulsion and consent, are
nowhere more blurred or more strenuously maintained
rhetorically than in the matter of Henry's betrothal to

Katherine. Henry V ratifies his lineal right to the French crown through the blood-rite of battle, yet his victory is not complete until he secures Katherine as his wife. Marriage to the French princess is vital to Henry's strategy of legitimation, as it enables this dubious claimant to the English throne to reappropriate the female lineage that is the true source of his claim to be the lawful king of France. Possessing Katherine as his wife will be to no purpose, however, if it does not secure Henry's place in the succession to the French crown, hence his rejection of Katherine's hand in marriage when it was offered, together with 'Some petty and unprofitable dukedoms' as dowry, earlier in the play (III.Chorus.29–32). After Agincourt Katherine becomes his 'capital demand' (V.2. 96), but in place of the proffered dukedoms he demands that he be proclaimed '*Héritier de France*', the immediate successor to the French throne (V.2.328–34). The marriage, like the peace, must be made on the conqueror's terms.

Henry's possession of Katherine is a metonym for his possession of France, as the King of France is well aware. When Henry reminds the French court that they should be thankful that he has been blinded by love, the French king dismisses Henry's romantic pretence. Rather than being so blinded by infatuation that he 'cannot see many a fair French city for one fair French maid' (V.2.312–13) Henry sees them 'perspectively, the cities turned into a maid' (315–16). The accuracy of this observation is made plain when the King of France seeks to preserve his country's honour in defeat by affirming that, just as his daughter's chastity is intact, so too many French cities remain 'girdled with maiden walls, that war hath never entered' (316–17). Henry's reply is blunt: French cities may keep their 'maiden walls' so long as Katherine ceases

to be a maid and becomes his wife, 'so the maiden cities
you talk of may wait on her: so the maid that stood in
the way for my wish shall show me the way to my will'
(320–22). Sexual penetration of Katherine's virginal body
in the expectation she shall 'prove a good soldier-breeder'
and 'compound a boy . . . that shall . . . take the Turk by
the beard' (203–7) and matrimonial possession of her
royal genealogy on terms that make Henry next in line
to the French crown do not mark Henry's relinquishment
of his wider war aims; they are the means by which those
war aims are secured – or so he hopes.

The King of France does not ask his daughter whether
she is willing to marry the King of England and he agrees
to the match offstage while she is onstage with Henry
(V.2.326). By contrast, Henry repeatedly asks Katherine
'will you have me?' (231–2, 243), yet his comic-romantic
bid for her consent is prefaced by his bald statement that
France 'must buy' the peace it seeks and the princess is
his 'capital demand' (V.2.70, 96). Consent expressed
under compulsion is not consent. Pressed for an answer
by her suitor, Katherine eventually responds 'Dat is as it
shall please de *Roi mon père*' (V.2.244). The princess
frames her conditional consent ('Den it sall also content
me', 247) as an act of obedience to her king and father,
not as an expression of affection much less love for 'de
ennemi of *France*' (168–9). Katherine and Henry both
know that Agincourt has sealed her fate, a fact that
Henry's decision to imitate the bluff manner of Hotspur,
court Katherine as 'plain soldier' (V.2.148–9) and rename
her English 'Kate' implicitly acknowledges. By addressing
Katherine informally by the common English diminutive
Henry domesticates the French princess, much as
Petruccio asserts his mastery of Katherine Minola in *The
Taming of the Shrew* by addressing her as 'plain Kate' in

defiance of her wishes (II.1.185). The victor at Agincourt does not need Katherine's consent, yet he persistently seeks it; he is not compelled to extend the prospect of mutual empery, and yet he does. One moment he is the triumphant conqueror speaking unnervingly like Tamburlaine – 'I love France so well that I will not part with a village of it – I will have it all mine' (V.2.172–3); the next he urges Katherine to 'Put off [her] maiden blushes', assume 'the looks of an empress' and receive all that he possesses:

> take me by the hand, and say, 'Harry of England, I am thine': which word thou shalt no sooner bless mine ear withal but I will tell thee aloud, 'England is thine, Ireland is thine, France is thine, and Henry Plantagenet is thine' . . . (V.2.232–8)

The virile conqueror invites the conquered woman to become 'Queen of all' (242), thus does Henry walk a rhetorical tightrope between the fact of compulsion and the semblance of consent and companionate marriage. The gesture is attractive, as is Henry's self-deprecating humour. Within moments, however, the victor at Agincourt betrays his imperiousness when he spurns French custom and insists that Katherine submit, 'patiently, and yielding' (271), to a maiden kiss on the lips, after which she falls silent.

Throughout their encounter Katherine speaks in French or 'broken English' (243), a trait that sets her apart from virtually all of the other speakers in the play. With the exception of the cowardly Le Fer and his translator, the soon-to-be-slaughtered Boy, the men typically speak English regardless of their nationality, as does Isabel, whereas Alice and Katherine typically speak

French. Henry's utterance of a few halting words in French is consistent with his tactful efforts to bridge the differences between himself and his future bride by disclaiming his eloquence. Katherine's language lesson in Act III, scene 4 has the opposite effect: instead of diminishing her marginalization, it intensifies her subjection to a foreign language that strips her of authority. The placement of her lesson immediately after the surrender of Harfleur aligns Katherine's need to learn English (III.4.4–5) with Henry's deepening incursion into France. Her halting acquisition of the conqueror's language takes the form of naming parts of her body, a process that sees Katherine unknowingly translate her chaste body into a bawdy register. Englishing her body doubly debases the French princess, first, by associating her with the brothel-keeping Hostess Quickly, whose comic idiom is the unwitting obscenity, and, second, by figuratively undressing and sexualizing parts of her anatomy in a titillating linguistic striptease conducted in the presence of male playgoers. The sexual connotations of 'Englishing' a woman's body are established in *The Merry Wives of Windsor* when Falstaff boasts that 'to be Englished rightly', what Alice Ford's 'familiar style' towards him denotes is: '"I am Sir John Falstaff's".' Pistol observes that Falstaff has 'translated her will, out of honesty, into English' (I.3.43–4). This sense of Englishing as rendering unchaste may inflect Burgundy's question, 'teach you our Princess English?' (V.2.278), when the sudden re-entrance of the negotiators causes Henry hurriedly to part from kissing Katherine in violation of French decorum. The debasing effects of Katherine's Englishing are apparent when her virginity becomes the subject of coarse sexual banter between Burgundy and Henry conducted in her presence.

In a scene in which Henry is addressed as 'England', France is feminized, peace is personified as a poor naked woman and Katherine is silenced, the relationship between the dynamics of invasion and possession and the martial and sexual mastery of the foreign, feminine and female are all too plain (unless we choose not to note them). It is little wonder, then, that the one unquestionable 'testament of noble-ending love' (IV.6.27) in *Henry V* is not that between Henry and Katherine but that between York and Suffolk, two men 'espoused to death' (26). York's final tender embrace and dying kiss on the lips of Suffolk are loving and unforced. The Epilogue reminds us that Henry's attempt to bring his policy of war to a comic close did not succeed. Peace did not last, the enmity between France and England which he had reignited was not extinguished by his marriage, and his fame did not secure the lineal transmission of either the crown of France or the crown of England to his son. '[T]he world's best garden' (7) was despoiled to no lasting purpose.

PERSPECTIVISM

In *Richard III* Prince Edward asks Buckingham whether Julius Caesar built the Tower of London. Buckingham's matter-of-fact reply, 'He did, my gracious lord, begin that place | Which since succeeding ages have re-edified' (III.1.70–71), does not satisfy the young prince, who presses Buckingham to clarify whether he bases his assertion on written records or on an oral tradition 'reported | Successively from age to age' (72–3). Edward believes 'the truth should live from age to age ... Even to the general all-ending day' (76–8). An idealist, he will soon be dead: his ambitious uncle shall see to it that the proverbial saying 'So wise so young ... do never live long' (III.1.79) holds true by suborning his murder and that of his young brother in the Tower. For Prince Edward history and truth should be unitary and immutable and the spoken word sufficient to ensure that past events are reported accurately to succeeding generations.

The past, however, is not a unified, stable entity that historians, archaeologists, literary scholars and the like can recover wholesale and reconstitute in the form of a single objective narrative. It is endlessly 're-edified' by succeeding ages. On the night before the battle of Agincourt three common soldiers enter into a heated debate with a stranger about the morality of war and the responsibility carried by those who order men into battle. One, suggestively surnamed Williams, mocks the disguised king's intimation that there is anything 'that a poor and a private displeasure can do against a monarch' (IV.1.193–4). Unlike his king, who gives Williams's glove to Fluellen as a prank, Williams keeps his word to challenge whoever bears his gage. When he learns that it was his king with whom he had violently quarrelled Williams defends his conduct: 'had you been as I took you for, I made no offence' (IV.8.54–5) – sight too can prove deceptive. We never learn of the fate of John Bates and Alexander Court. In performance only 'Brother John Bates' (IV.1.84) is addressed by name and the king does not enquire after their identities. Are they among the twenty-five 'other men' deemed not to be 'of name' (IV.8.104–5) listed among the English dead? As *Henry V* persistently reminds us, there is more than one way of remembering the past and more than one history to be remembered. Like history, Shakespeare's play is multivalent and perspectival. Which version of the play directors choose to stage, which version of events we choose to remember, and which of the many perspectives on Henry and his wars we allow to inform – and challenge – our understanding is ultimately a matter of judgement. However, those seeking a straightforwardly patriotic war play and an uncomplicatedly heroic and pious English national hero should look elsewhere than to the 'long' Folio version of *Henry V* for their entertainment.

Ann Kaegi

The Play in Performance

Performing a play that was written over four centuries ago presents its own set of challenges. Several features of *Henry V* that would have excited the interest of play-goers in Shakespeare's day now distance audiences from his drama. When the play was first staged the 'famous victories' achieved by Henry V in France continued to be memorialized in chronicles, ballads, stage plays and poems, ensuring that the martial exploits of England's warrior king remained the stuff of popular legend. However, for the overwhelming majority of those who encounter *Henry V* in the twenty-first century the once celebrated names of Crécy and Agincourt, Edward III and the Black Prince, not to mention King Harry, have long ceased to be as 'Familiar ... as household words' (IV.3.52). The ancient rivalry between England and France may not be wholly extinguished, but it retains little of its former fervency. The passage of time has also ensured that what had once been a highly topical allusion to the Irish expedition of the Earl of Essex in the fifth chorus (29–35) is now routinely cut in performance. Meantime, as a consequence of changing usage, once familiar words and expressions have fallen out of currency, altering for ever our relationship to the play's language.

While some elements of *Henry V* have lost something of their former immediacy, the capacity of other elements of the play to engage and provoke audiences remains undiminished by time and may even be enhanced as a consequence of wider cultural and historical developments. Several late-twentieth- and early-twenty-first-century productions of *Henry V* on stage and screen have sought to supplement those elements of Shakespeare's play that lend it an arresting contemporaneity by adopting costumes and set designs that evoke more recent military conflicts, such as the Vietnam War, the war over the Falkland/Malvinas islands, the civil wars that destroyed Yugoslavia, the first Gulf War, and the invasions of Afghanistan and Iraq. By providing modern visual equivalents to the verbal intrusion into *Henry V* of the intensifying conflict in Ireland and the lingering fear of a Spanish invasion such 'presentist' productions seek to recapture something of the topical resonance of the original. More importantly, recent military conflicts and the controversies surrounding them have lent those passages that associate warfare variously with greed and deception, rape, massacre and ecological disaster a renewed urgency. The continuing resonance of these speeches is all the more disturbing for the passage of time. Because it was thought to detract from the depiction of Henry V as a heroic figure worthy of emulation and his invasion of France as an ennobling enterprise worthy of celebration, this disquieting material was routinely omitted from productions of *Henry V* until well into the twentieth century. Although contemporary practice varies widely, a rising proportion of productions have opted to retain it. Hopefully this trend signals a greater willingness to confront rather than circumvent the play's many and profound challenges in performance. This section highlights several of those challenges and briefly examines how different performance options may affect key elements of the play.

'THEN BROOK ABRIDGEMENT'
(V.CHORUS.44)

With the publication of modern editions of the first Quarto of *Henry V*, directors have a choice of two distinct versions of the play on which to base their production. As noted in the Introduction (pp. xxv–xxvii), the first Quarto and the first Folio offer not just different but essentially opposing representations of Henry V and his French campaign, so a pick-and-mix approach is best avoided. At around 3,400 lines the first Folio version (1623), on which this edition is based, is one of the longest Shakespearian play texts; at just over 1,620 lines the first Quarto text (1600) is one of the shortest. If a swiftly paced war play that largely favours an idealized interpretation of the warrior king is desired, then the Quarto is the better option. If a more testing theatrical experience is sought, then the Folio text, with its sudden swings from loftiness to lowliness, from grandiose myth-making to chilling realpolitik, supplies the more challenging acoustic, emotional and moral landscape for performers and audiences to navigate. This section on the play in performance is concerned with productions of the Folio text.

With its running time of just under four hours, directors who opt for the Folio version must decide whether and if so how best to make cuts. The existence of the first Quarto (the only version printed in Shakespeare's lifetime) may indicate that even the play's first audiences were thought to lack the stamina (or the stomach) for the 'long' version. Among the longer, and in certain instances more readerly, passages in the Folio text that rarely survive intact are Canterbury's exposition of the Salic law (I.2.33–95), Henry's denunciation of Scroop (II.2.79–144), the once topical and now dated reference to 'the General ... from Ireland coming' (V.Chorus.29–35), Henry's courtship of Katherine, and Burgundy's description of the devastating effects of war on 'Our fertile France' (V.2.23–67) together with his sexually mocking exchange with Henry (277–310).

With the exception of the Essex allusion, the above passages illustrate the care that must be taken in making extensive cuts to the Folio text to quicken the tempo. Tampering with Canterbury's lengthy commentary on the Salic law is particularly hazardous as it sets out the legal justification for Henry's war, while it also subtly draws attention to Henry's tainted title as King of England. Canterbury's assertion that his laboured exposition is 'as clear as is the summer's sun' (I.2.86) usually draws audience laughter; however, trimming the speech to make it clearer presupposes that the legitimacy of Henry's claim to the French crown is meant to appear unambiguous. A large onstage map is sometimes used to clarify Canterbury's contention that the Salic lands (to which the law barring female inheritance applies) lie in Germany not France. His second line of argument consists of citing historical precedents for Henry's claim through the female line, but these precedents are potentially damning as each is characterized by Canterbury as a usurper or the son of a usurper. If the actor emphasizes the words 'deposèd' (65), 'usurped' (69) and 'usurper' (78), their dubiousness and Henry's similarly suspect status as the son of a usurper of the English throne edge into view. If Henry's protracted denunciation of

Scroop is omitted, then the thematic parallel between the king's betrayal by his former bedfellow and his own responsibility for hastening the death of Falstaff is lost. Yet if Henry's long-winded attack on Scroop is not shortened, not only does the opening sequence lose momentum but his sustained reproof may further obscure the political motive for the conspiracy (its likely purpose) and also crowd out the audience's recollection that 'The King hath run bad humours on the knight' (II.1.116), Sir John Falstaff, who had been as a father to him.

In the Quarto text Henry persuades the Governor of Harfleur to surrender with a twelve-line speech and polishes off his courtship of Katherine in less than a third the time it takes in the Folio text. The rapidity of the former makes him appear militarily indomitable while the brevity of the latter fosters the impression that he is romantically irresistible. In the Folio text his assault on Harfleur encounters military setbacks and his love suit meets with linguistic setbacks. Henry eventually wins the French town with words; do his words win over the French princess and could he not 'speak fewer' (IV.1.65)? The analogy between Henry's prospective siege of 'many a fair French city' and his attempted seduction of 'one fair French maid' is made explicit by both Henry and the French king in the Folio text (V.2.311–17). Compressing his courtship is therefore consequential, though possibly less critical than are cuts to Katherine's remarks in French and broken English (the Quarto retains only one) as they establish that her grasp of the conqueror's language is extremely limited. Unlike *The Famous Victories of Henry the fifth*, where Katherine is plainly keen to wed Henry, in Shakespeare the responses of the French princess to 'de *ennemi* of *France*' (V.2.168–9) are invariably guarded; however, if the actor playing Katherine appears to be won by Henry's torrent of speech, then her efforts to deflect his suit will be interpreted as coyness or coquettishness. Audiences who witness Emma Thompson's Katherine leaning forward to be kissed by Kenneth Branagh's Henry V in close up in his 1989 film are likely to overlook the fact that, textually, Katherine's replies to Henry in the Folio are consistently restrained and noncommittal and are often uncomprehending.

Should Burgundy's framing commentaries on Henry's 'victories' be sacrificed to inject some momentum into the closing sequence? His speech describing the devastation caused by Henry's invasion is a moving indictment of war delivered in the aftermath of Henry's most celebrated victory, while his provocatively cynical sexual banter with Henry imparts a very different gloss to the conqueror's 'courtship' of the French princess (see Introduction, p. lxxiv). Burgundy's contributions to the closing scene challenge audiences to reflect more deeply on the nature of Henry's twin triumphs; if they are omitted, the pace quickens but the play's internal critique of the celebrated history it stages is greatly diminished. The Folio text can 'brook abridgement' but, as these examples demonstrate, cuts to the text need to be done with a scalpel, not an axe.

'ADMIT ME CHORUS TO THIS HISTORY' (PROLOGUE.32)

The hallmark of the Folio text is its extraordinary generic and tonal hybridity and the rapidity with which genre and tone change and often collide. A key source of that hybridity and one of the trickiest elements of the play to accommodate is the Chorus. Stirring, yet at times wildly inaccurate, should the Chorus (absent from the first Quarto along with the Prologue and Epilogue) be kept or jettisoned? And if it is retained, should its speeches be reworked to eliminate the jarring discontinuities between the choric narrative and the ensuing action outlined in the Introduction (pp. xliii–li)? Few decisions will have a greater impact on the tenor of a Folio-based production of _Henry V_ than these. David Giles, director of the 1979 BBC television film of _Henry V_, put the case for retaining the Chorus succinctly: 'If you cut the Chorus, you don't do _Henry V_' (quoted in Loehlin, _Shakespeare in Performance: 'Henry V_', p. 75), or at least not the Folio version. How far, though, should the discontinuities between the choric account and the subsequent action be allowed to undermine the credibility of the heroic legend the Chorus celebrates? Many directors move the announcement by the second chorus of the shift of scene to Southampton to the beginning of Act II, scene 2. Omitting or transposing portions of the other choruses can similarly make them accord with rather than misrepresent the dramatic action. (Laurence Olivier's changes resulted in the creation of ten Chorus speeches in his 1944 film in place of the original six.) Alternatively, Ron Daniels (for the Royal Shakespeare Company in 1997) ensured that as the fourth chorus invited the audience to 'behold | The royal Captain ... Walking from watch to watch' dispensing 'A little touch of Harry in the night' (28–47) Henry could be seen behind a gauze curtain walking among his men precisely as described. Modifying the choruses to eliminate inconsistencies between what the Chorus encourages audiences to anticipate and what happens next presumes that existing discrepancies are errors that should be corrected in performance.

Others note that the Chorus is consistently wrong and

its mis-statements of fact are therefore unlikely to be over-sights. Rather than reconfigure its speeches to make the Chorus appear trustworthy, they elect to do the opposite and draw attention to the discrepancies between the Chorus's announcements and the subsequent action. The layout of the Elizabethan public stage, with its openings flanking and (often) at the centre of the back wall, facil-itated both continuous action and dramatic juxtapositions through the use of overlapping entrances and exits. If Nym and Bardolph enter arguing as the Act II Chorus is still making his (or her) exit, as happened in Richard Olivier's 1997 production at the reconstructed Globe Theatre, the unreliability of the Chorus is vividly apparent. In theatres where the size or configuration of the stage makes it difficult for audiences to detect such overlaps, dumb shows or static tableaux can intensify the audience's perception of the falsity of the Chorus's historical account. In his 2003 production in the cavernous Olivier Theatre, Nicholas Hytner had the Act II Chorus announce centre stage that 'all the youth of England are on fire' (1) while Nym, seated upstage in a 'pub', used a television remote to flick idly between a broadcast by Henry, an interview with Canterbury and assorted sporting fixtures until, visibly bored by the offerings, he switched the set off as the Chorus affirmed 'now sits expec-tation in the air' (8). Another option is to sharpen the rivalry between the heroic and anti-heroic voices in the play. In Giles's television film the camera pulls back to reveal the Chorus unknowingly standing nose to nose with Bardolph; startled, the Chorus hastily retreats. Terry Hands went a step further in his 1975 RSC production and had Bardolph and Nym interrupt the Chorus as he spoke of 'English Mercuries' (7), forcing him to give way to their anti-heroic ribaldry with a resigned shrug; only after their departure did the Chorus reappear to announce the shift of scene. Perhaps the Chorus is merely indulging the habit of 'remember[ing], with advantages' (IV.3.50) to which we are all susceptible. By having a different cast member speak each chorus Richard Olivier transformed the choric narrative into a collaborative account that recorded how key participants wished to be remembered (a device previously adopted in a 1957 production at the Library Theatre, Manchester).

Harry's observation that 'Old men forget' (IV.3.49) provides another explanation for the Chorus's faulty memory. Just how old *is* the Chorus? Advancing age might account for the sense of loss and nostalgic yearning that pervades the choruses; alternatively, youth – earnest, eager, unbloodied – might explain their zealous idealization of Henry V and war and reinforce the contrast with the prematurely knowing Boy, particularly if the same actor plays both parts. When *Henry V* is performed as part of a sequence of histories there is scope for inventive doubling across the series. John Woodvine, who had played Falstaff, reappeared as the Chorus in Michael Bogdanov's touring production of the *Richard II* to *Henry V* sequence (English Shakespeare Company, 1986–9), deftly fulfilling the pledge in the Epilogue to *Henry IV, Part II* to 'continue the story, with Sir John in it' (27) while accentuating the contrast between Falstaff's loyalty to Hal and Hal's public spurning of the 'fat knight with the great-belly doublet' (IV.7.46). And what about a female Chorus? The scarcity of female roles in *Henry V* can be slightly allayed by casting women in non-speaking roles or transformed by having an all-female cast, an option some theatre companies resorted to during the two world wars. It can also be mitigated by having a female Chorus, a practice that was widely adopted from the mid nineteenth century until the 1930s and shows signs of a moderate comeback. Formerly women Choruses personified an abstraction such as Britannia or Clio, the Muse of history. In 1872 Mrs Charles Calvert spoke the Prologue as 'Rumour' from *Henry IV, Part II*, accoutred with a golden horn. More unusually, a cross-dressed Sybil Thorndike reversed the practice of female impersonation on the all-male stage of Shakespeare's day by performing Chorus as an Elizabethan boy (at the Lyric, Hammersmith, 1927–8), suggesting how a woman too might double the roles of Chorus and Boy. The growing numbers of women in a greater range of employment allows for a wider variety of depictions. With half-moon reading specs perched on her nose, Penny Downie's hero-worshipping Chorus in Hytner's modern-dress production was characterized by one reviewer as 'an insinuating spin-doctor in high heels' (*Observer*, 18 May 2003) and by another as 'sounding like a cross between a condescending *Newsnight* compere and a literature don lecturing to fairly thick students' (*Evening Standard*, 14 May 2003).

Costuming can clarify the relationship of the Chorus to the play. The Chorus's fondness for rhetorical flourishes can be mocked or indulged by portraying him or her as a flamboyant figure in dandyish modern or Elizabethan dress (as in Laurence Olivier's 1944 film or Peter Hall and John Barton's production in 1964). Is the Chorus a detached observer or an actual or vicarious participant in the drama? Portraying the Chorus as Britannia, Clio, 'Time' (complete with scythe and hourglass) like the choric figure in *The Winter's Tale* (William Macready in 1839 and Samuel Phelps in 1852) or Shakespeare (as happened in the wartime Shakespeare Birthday Celebrations in April 1943) lends the Chorus considerable authority. Such depictions also emphasize the Chorus's detachment from the dramatic action, as does the option of having the Chorus wear modern dress while the other actors wear period costume or vice versa. Modern dress enables the insinuating Chorus to appear as a disarming intermediary between the audience and the play. Branagh wanted the Chorus in his film to be an 'everyman' figure. While the rest of the cast wear medieval garb, Derek Jacobi as Chorus wears a modern, nondescript overcoat and a red scarf wrapped loosely around his neck, his anachronistic and slightly 'actorly' appearance serving as a constant reminder both of the filmic dimension and of his (and our) historical remove from the events being portrayed – that is until he appears with a grimy face and grazed forehead bearing visible marks of battle! Costuming the Chorus in military attire further blurs the distinction between the roles of participant and observer. An anachronistically overcoated Chorus reappeared in Mathew Warchus's 1994 RSC version, but the addition of a Remembrance Day poppy and campaign ribbons, complemented by his upright military bearing, conveyed that the elderly Chorus was a war veteran, a fellowship in arms that was reinforced when he assisted Henry to his feet during the battle for Agincourt.

Young or old, male or female, modern or period dress, what matters is that the Chorus is understood by directors to be engaged in a struggle to fashion remembrance. What directors decide to do with the Chorus can tip the balance in the contest to control whose story is told and how the past is remembered that lies at the heart of the Folio version. If the choruses are left in place and no attempt is made to mask the glaring inconsistencies between what the Chorus reports and the ensuing action, a production based on the Folio text will feature acute shifts in tone, from epic to comic, from hyperbolic verse to plain-speaking prose, and in historical remembrance from the promotion of a legend to its abrupt demystification. The first Quarto provides a precedent for those who wish to dispense with the services of the Chorus, Prologue and Epilogue. If the director's aim is to represent Henry V and his victory at Agincourt as a model of greatness, then performance history suggests that the choruses will need to be selectively edited, transposed or dropped. If the intent is to explore in collaboration with the audience how such martial legends are 'perfected' and the harsh truths they obscure, then the choruses are best kept in place.

'FOUR OR FIVE MOST VILE AND RAGGED FOILS' (IV.CHORUS.50)

If the Chorus's speeches are preserved, directors face the daunting prospect of beginning the performance with a prologue that anticipates that the 'unworthy scaffold' (10) of the commercial theatre (or film set) will inevitably debase 'So great an object' (11) as 'warlike Harry' (5) and his memorable triumph at Agincourt. As for the actors or 'ciphers to this great account' (17), the fourth chorus glumly predicts that they will 'much disgrace, | With four or five most vile and ragged foils, | Right ill-disposed in brawl ridiculous, | The name of Agincourt' (IV. Chorus.49–52). The intrusively non-naturalistic Chorus reminds audiences that what they are witnessing is a play, that the people on stage are actors and that the theatre has limited powers of representation. How best to respond? Olivier and Branagh both opted to emphasize this quality of self-reflexivity at the outset of their respective *Henry V* films, Branagh by having the Chorus speak straight to camera as he leads the viewer through a film studio on to the sound stage and 'into' the film, and Olivier by first transporting viewers across Elizabethan London to the Globe Theatre where a performance of *The Chronicle History of King Henry the Fift'* is about to begin. Our first glimpse of Henry V is of the actor clearing his throat backstage as he awaits his cue. In Hands's 1975 RSC production actors milled about the stage in rehearsal clothes as audience members found their seats and only relinquished their everyday outfits after the French Ambassador arrived in 'period' costume with the Chorus remaining in 'rehearsal' clothes throughout. Such devices foreground the performance medium and its conventions and may prompt audiences to consider the extent to which Henry's authority (and legendary stature) is similarly a theatrical and rhetorical construction.

Directors who try to rebut the Chorus by exploiting all available resources to create realist or stylized spectacle accord the audience a lesser role than it is allocated by the Chorus. The Prologue shifts responsibility for ensuring Henry V and his famous victories assume epic stature decisively away from the 'wooden O' (13) of the theatre and the 'crookèd figure' (15) of the actor to the audience's 'imaginary forces' (18). However, many directors are reluctant to entrust such a crucial task of 'imaginary puissance' (25) to the audience and are disinclined to restrain the impulse to confect a 'swelling scene' (4) on stage or screen, since it obliges them to jettison treasured assumptions about what a play about Henry V and Agincourt should look like. Despite the Chorus's apologetic insistence that the performance doesn't remotely resemble the majestic scenes it urges us to imagine, lavish spectacle, pageantry and vast numbers of supernumeraries were characteristic features of eighteenth- and nineteenth-century productions. As Olivier's and Branagh's films attest, Harfleur and Agincourt are still prone to becoming occasions for elaborate military spectacle in modern productions. Having adopted a 'found space aesthetic' that entailed stripping the Olivier stage back to its architectural frame, Hytner broke with that aesthetic to incorporate realist military spectacles: instead of audiences imagining horses 'Printing their proud hoofs i'th'receiving earth' (Prologue.27), two military Land Rovers, complete with mounted machine guns, were driven on and off the stage during battle sequences accompanied by smoke and the sound of modern ordnance, while actors dressed in military fatigues and bearing realistic weapons used actual military tactics to move across the stage. It is not a lack of extras and realistic weaponry, however, that risks making Agincourt appear a 'brawl ridiculous' but rather Shakespeare's audacious decision to limit the depiction of the celebrated battle to an encounter between two misapprehending cowards and a scene of French confusion (Act IV, scenes 4 and 5), and to restrict the display of Henry's generalship once combat has commenced to an order to kill defenceless prisoners (IV.6.37) and a renewed threat to 'cut the throats of those we have' (IV.7.61) when he spies French horsemen on a nearby hill. Staging this version as distinct from the legend requires few resources except courage.

On the subject of courage, the most controversial material in the Folio text continues to test the mettle of directors. Ron Daniels (RSC, 1997) and Nicholas Hytner (National Theatre, 2003) are among a minority of directors to preserve Henry's cruellest threats to the citizens of Harfleur in Act III, scene 3, for example. Most directors, from Kemble in the eighteenth century through to Branagh in the twentieth, have tended to make heavy cuts similar to those in the Quarto (which omits lines 11–41) to prevent Henry's graphic threats from tarnishing his heroic and pious image. However, unlike the historical sources, which report that Henry V sacked Harfleur, in Shakespeare Henry's threatening speech is exposed as a ruse moments after the town surrenders and can be played up as such. Michael Pennington (ESC, 1986–9) whistled with amazement when his gambit succeeded; Branagh 'closes his eyes in exhaustion and relief' in his film version (*Beginning*, p. 60); and both drew attention to the sickness spreading through Henry's army (III.3.55–6) by betraying signs of illness as the scene ended, giving the lie to the terrifying vision of 'th'enragèd soldiers in their spoil' (25) Henry had evoked in his speech.

If Henry's famous rallying speech at Harfleur and his most savage menaces are retained (both are absent from the Quarto) to whom should they be directed? The carrying on of scaling-ladders (III.1.0) suggests that in Shakespeare's theatre the attack on the breach was directed at the back wall of the stage, with the Governor appearing on its balcony. The audience would then view the attack from the conqueror's (and the Eastcheapers') perspective. Daniels and Hytner opted to have Henry address both his battle oration urging his soldiers to advance 'Once more unto the breach' (III.1.1) and his speech threatening total war to the audience, with the soldiers in Hytner's production 'entering' Harfleur by advancing up the aisles, making Henry's terror tactics all the more palpable. The audience thus experienced the attack on Harfleur from the dual perspectives of the town's attackers and its defenders, significantly complicating their response to Henry's 'victory'.

Unlike Henry's speech threatening the citizens of Harfleur with total war, the execution of Bardolph is not a bluff. By substituting Bardolph for the unnamed soldier recorded in the sources and by making it plain that Henry could yet intervene to save his former companion, who is still alive but 'like to be executed' by Exeter (III.6.97–8), Shakespeare generates what can be a defining moment in the characterization of the king – and of Pistol. Henry's tactical calculation that 'when lenity and cruelty play for a kingdom, the gentler gamester is the soonest winner' (109–10) puts productions that emphasize the king's heroism and piety under acute strain. David Gwilliam (BBC, 1979) brought out the hollowness of Henry's espousals of fellowship and bravely risked audience sympathy by coldly pronouncing Bardolph's death sentence, 'We would have all such offenders so cut off' (104–5), after a considered pause from polishing his boots. By contrast, Alan Howard (RSC, 1975) portrayed Henry's seemingly impersonal response to Bardolph's offstage execution as a painful emotional ordeal for the king, as does a tearful Branagh as he watches Bardolph hanged in his film version. Instead of emphasizing Henry's pain, Bogdanov (ESC, 1986–9) and Michael Boyd (RSC, 2007) both emphasized Pistol's desperate efforts to save his friend, with Pistol braving sniper and mortar fire in Boyd's production in a fruitless attempt to persuade Fluellen to intervene on Bardolph's behalf. Pistol's steadfast fellowship sharply contrasted with Henry's ruthlessness and increasing isolation in these versions.

Those who wish to endorse Henry's attribution of the historic victory at Agincourt to divine intervention will be strongly tempted to follow Olivier and Branagh in omitting Henry's command to kill the French prisoners (IV.6.37). If it is kept, should the audience witness the massacre? 'Give the word through' (38) implies the killing occurs offstage, a pragmatic solution that avoids the need to drag off several bodies. Boyd solved the staging problem by using smoke, sound and lighting effects to create the impression the French prisoners were being burnt alive in a pit beneath the stage. In the Quarto Pistol (present but silent until now) responds to Henry's order with his catchphrase, 'Couple gorge'. Productions that adopt the Quarto line typically have Pistol kill Le Fer on stage, often under compulsion as Pistol's hopes of profiting from Henry's wars die with his captive. Having Fluellen reprise his role at the breach and compel Pistol's compliance foregrounds the increasingly bitter relationship between the two. Kevin Kline displayed a willingness to sacrifice audience sympathy rare among performers of the title role by personally cutting Le Fer's throat when he played Henry V in the 1984 Central Park production. Warchus too took the unusual step of involving the king in the killing by having Henry physically force Pistol's sword across Le Fer's throat (RSC, 1994). Another consideration is what, if any, causal relation Henry's order should have to the French raid on the boys guarding the luggage wagons. Gower wrongly assumes that Henry's command was in revenge for the cowardly French raid when, textually, it precedes it (IV.7.5–10). By reversing the dramatic sequence to make Gower's misconstruction appear correct Hands glossed over Henry's most chilling act of pragmatism in the play. The widespread practice of showing the killing of the boys in dumb show, as in Adrian Noble's 1984 RSC version, or of bearing the body of the Boy on stage may prompt audiences to forget the actual sequence of events, particularly if the killing of the French prisoners is not shown. If both massacres are accorded equal prominence, the horror of war 'That makes such waste in brief mortality' (I.2.28) is impressed on the audience as the battle of Agincourt staggers to a gruesome and unseemly close.

Less gruesome episodes, such as Henry's quarrel with Bates and Williams and its aftermath, can be defining moments in a production, particularly as their quarrel centres on the king's moral responsibilities towards his subjects when he wages war. Does Williams accept Henry's offer of the glove filled with crowns, or does he dare to reject it? If the latter, the king would presumably need to respond, yet neither speaks to the other after it is offered. If he accepts the gift of crowns, does he do so happily, relieved to extricate himself from the quarrel and its hazards? Or does Williams accept the glove grudgingly because he must, since 'to disobey were against all proportion of subjection' (IV.1.141–2). And does he continue to refuse Fluellen's offer of a shilling to mend his shoes because he can express his anger openly to the Welsh captain whereas he could not spurn the king, or are they too reconciled?

How the opposing parties to the conflict in France are portrayed can significantly sway audience sympathies for or against war, Henry and the French. Speakers on both sides, not least Henry himself, emphasize the starkly contrasting appearance of the two forces. The Chorus could hardly be characterized as unbiased, but its appraisal of the French as 'Proud ... secure ... confident and over-lusty' (IV.Chorus.17–18) before Agincourt is fair. The same Chorus describes Henry's army as a 'ruined band' (29) whose 'lank-lean cheeks and war-worn coats' (26) lend them the appearance of 'So many horrid ghosts' (28), as if the dead of the preceding history plays had been conjured back to life for one last battle. In the early nineteenth century when Napoleon threatened invasion productions pandered to jingoist anti-French sentiment by depicting the French as effete dandies. Just as costuming and set design can reinforce a derogatory national stereotype, they can also be used to reverse or unseat it. Rather than staging Act II, scene 4 as a formal council scene, Bogdanov's production showed the French court in their first appearance enjoying a summer luncheon: the men, dressed in white linen and seated downstage on white garden chairs, sipped wine as they evaluated the English threat while the women picnicked upstage, until Exeter brusquely strode across their white picnic blanket in his dark diplomat's suit and red sash to deliver Henry's imperialist threat of 'Bloody constraint' (II.4.97), abruptly shattering the Impressionist idyll. So striking and persistent were the contrasts between dignified French civility and xenophobic British warmongering (a banner proclaiming 'Fuck the French' was draped over the balcony as Henry embarked from Southampton) that one reviewer confessed it was 'the first version I've ever seen where you wanted the French to win' (*Guardian*, 23 March 1987). Whereas the entrances of both the English and French forces were occasions for historical pageantry on the Victorian stage, spectacle tends to be reserved for the French in modern productions in keeping with the preoccupation of the French peers with the accoutrements of their status: their noble lineages, their horses (and mistresses) and their armour. The vertical axis can be exploited to emphasize French hubris, as in Noble's production, where Henry's mud-splattered army entered at stage level while the French descended before Agincourt 'godlike, on golden tea-trays' (*Times Literary Supplement*, 13 April 1984), resplendent in their glistening armour, and Boyd's, where the French peers and their herald routinely appeared on trapezes, the exaggeratedly long tails of the peers' embroidered frock coats trailing beneath their languid forms until defeat at Agincourt brought them to ground. Costuming the French in historically outmoded dress and Henry's army in modern dress can illuminate why the devotion of the French peers to an outmoded medieval chivalric code results not only in their defeat at Agincourt but also in the disproportionate losses suffered by France.

Although historical pageantry is rare in modern productions, those that retain the play's most brutal episodes and utterances sometimes neuter much of their force by using vivid tableau staging and choreographed movements of military banners and soldiers to project warfare as having a savage beauty. More commonly, evocations of modern warfare – the muddy slaughter of the First World War, the hooding of prisoners and their handcuffing with plastic ties, the machine-gunning of opponents – are used to deglamorize war for a public familiar with television images of recent conflicts. Williams's vivid reminder of 'all those legs, and arms, and heads, chopped off in a battle' (IV.1.131–2) distils this sense of the dehumanizing brutality of armed conflict. Some productions, such as Noble's, combine elements of the two. Even when war is deglamorized, Henry and his victory are frequently still valorized by portraying the king as a remorseful and self-doubting insomniac who is struggling selflessly to cope with the burden of responsibility he has inherited with the crown.

'THIS STAR OF ENGLAND'
(EPILOGUE.6)

With over forty speaking roles the Folio text is ideally suited to ensemble performance. Directors operating on a limited budget must give careful consideration to the doubling (or more) of parts, a practice that provides actors the opportunity to demonstrate their versatility and audiences the added pleasure of detecting contrasts and connections between roles, such as those discussed in relation to the Chorus. *Henry V* can also serve as a potential 'star vehicle'. The title role provides the opportunity to be both an action hero (though more in word than in deed) and briefly a romantic lead. As Henry V speaks about a third of all lines (in both versions), nearly four times as many as any other speaker, the leading actor can dominate the production. Aged just twenty-four, Kenneth Branagh made his name in the part in Noble's 1984 RSC production, while Laurence Olivier's film version broke box office records and established the veteran British stage actor as a film star in the United States. To serve as a star vehicle the play requires judicious trimming and rejigging. As noted above, Henry's order to kill the French prisoners and his later threat to cut the throats of those that survive are hurdles that some actors shy from. If the production is merely a vehicle for the leading actor then the smaller parts suffer, but the play's performance history shows that roles such as Quickly, Pistol, Fluellen, Exeter, Montjoy, the Boy, Bates and Williams can make a significant impact with the right casting and directorial care. Even the virtually silent Alexander Court has made a lasting impression in productions where he appears to be visibly suffering from post-traumatic stress.

Since the rise of Stanislavskian 'method' acting, with its emphasis on character psychology and motivation, one limitation of the title role is that Henry V has only one, interrupted soliloquy, most of which is given over to a complaint about the burdens of office and a meditation on ceremony until, in a postscript, we glimpse

Henry's anxious 'sense of reckoning' for his father's crimes against Richard II (IV.1.282–98). The contrast to *Julius Caesar* and *Hamlet*, one possibly written within months and the other within a year of *Henry V*, is striking – Henry V is no Brutus much less a brooding Hamlet. Although the role of Henry V does not obviously lend itself to meditative introspection, this has not deterred some actors from seeking to project just such qualities on to the king. Despite the paucity of soliloquies, Kenneth Branagh discerned a 'sense of Hamletian doubt' running through the part (*Beginning*, p. 137). One method of portraying Henry V as a ruler beset by inner conflicts is to place particular emphasis on moments of moral crisis in the play, such as Henry's blunt query to Canterbury, 'May I with right and conscience make this claim?' (I.2.96), Scroop's intimate act of betrayal, the hanging of Bardolph, the quarrel with Williams and, of course, the divided soliloquy on the night before Agincourt. Alan Howard portrayed Henry V as a youthful and inexperienced king struggling with his conscience and the burdens of kingship in Hands's 1975 RSC production by expanding on Henry's preoccupation in his soliloquy with the responsibility placed 'Upon the King' (IV.1.223) at every opportunity afforded by the text. This approach is often adopted when *Henry V* is performed as part of a historical cycle that includes the two parts of *Henry IV*. When the actor playing the role of Henry V also plays the role of Hal he is able to depict the political maturation of the prince and his (possibly reluctant) adaptation to and adoption of his political responsibilities as heir to the throne. That said, Hal's speech in *Henry IV, Part I* when he sets out his political strategy (I.2.192–214) shows a prince whose immaturity is more apparent than real. Is Henry V a calculating Machiavel intent on distracting attention from his dubious claim to the English crown by following his father's advice to 'busy giddy minds | With foreign quarrels' (*Henry IV, Part II*, IV.5.213–14), or is he 'the mirror of all Christian kings' (II.Chorus.6) and the heroic 'model to [England's] inward greatness' (16) celebrated by the Chorus?

These are among the many questions each production of *Henry V* must tackle and for which the play supplies an array of performance options. The challenges the Folio version of *Henry V* presents to performers and audiences are frequently daunting, and the temptation may be to eliminate contradiction, smooth sharp swings in genre and tone, cut complexity, and underplay or remove controversial material. There is always the first Quarto version for those so inclined. But as Shakespeare appears to have had the courage to include these unsettling traits in a play about a celebrated national hero written at a time of war, avoiding the challenges of his heterodox drama seems both cowardly and uninventive.

Ann Kaegi

Further Reading

EDITIONS AND SOURCES

There are a good range of editions of *Henry V* available in the major Shakespeare series, including two modern editions of the first Quarto (Q1) and a parallel text edition of the first Folio version (F). J. H. Walter's Arden edition (Second Series, 1954) was the first comprehensively edited text of the play and as such provides the template for most modern editions. (It is also the most 'pro-Henry' of the lot.) The most recent Folio-based editions of *Henry V* include the Oxford edition by Gary Taylor (1984), the New Cambridge edition by Andrew Gurr (Second Series, 1992) and T. W. Craik's edition in the Arden Third Series (1995). Their introductions are very different, but each provides an informative commentary on the play, its context and sources, date of composition, and critical and performance histories. Reading all three would be a good groundwork exercise for any student of the play. Taylor's Oxford edition follows on from his *Three Studies in the Text of 'Henry V'* (1979), where he argues that Q1 is a somewhat garbled record of how the play was adapted and abridged for performance, 'probably in the provinces' (p. 39), by a reduced company of eleven players. He nonetheless makes a case in his introduction for adopting a textual variant from Q1, which has Pistol pronounce his catchphrase, 'Couple gorge', at the end of Act IV, scene 6 after Henry gives his order to kill the French prisoners, and incorporates several other significant Quarto variants in his Folio-based edition. Appendix F provides a helpful list of passages not included in Q1. Craik is especially strong on Shakespeare's extensive borrowings from Holinshed's *Chronicle* (see below), which he reproduces in the notes beneath the passages in *Henry V* to which they relate. This procedure illuminates Shakespeare's heavy reliance on Holinshed and how the playwright went about adapting (or simply pilfering) source material. Another feature of Craik's edition likely to appeal in the classroom is its inclusion of a reduced photographic facsimile of the British Library's copy of Q1 in an appendix, though the size and quality of the reproduction can make for difficult reading at times. Andrew Gurr is presently in the unique position of having edited both the F (1992) and Q1 (2000) versions of *Henry V*. Printed eight years apart, Gurr's two editions are meant to complement each other, yet they clearly chart an important shift in textual scholarship on the so-called 'bad' quartos. Prior to Graham Holderness and Brian Loughrey's edition of Q1 in the Shakespearean Originals: First Editions series (1993) all editions of *Henry V* since 1623 had been based on F, as Q1 had long been regarded as one of the 'Stolne and surreptitious copies' of Shakespeare's plays to which Heminges and Condell refer in their preface to the first Folio. In a dramatic departure from this long-held view, Gurr argues in the introduction to his edition of Q1 that the Quarto text 'offers the best evidence we have of what routinely happened to the scripts that the Shakespeare company bought from their resident playwright' (p. ix). Where Gurr affirms the merits of Q1 as a record of how Shakespeare's scripts were radically altered for performance, Holderness and Loughrey argue that Q1 is worthy of critical attention and performance in its own right 'as a vigorous and powerful instance of Elizabethan comic-historical drama' (p. 13). Their approach is 'to essay comparisons between Quarto and Folio on the assumption of textual multiplicity and equivalence, as distinct from the tradition of interpretation predicated on the Quarto's self-evident inferiority' (pp. 22–3). A facsimile of Q1 can be found in *Shakespeare's Plays in Quarto*, edited by Michael Allen and Kenneth Muir (1981). In addition to the Folio-based editions of *Henry V* already discussed, F can also be accessed in a parallel text edition, *Henry V/The Life of Henry the Fift*, edited by Nick de Somogyi (2001), in The Shakespeare Folios series, which prints the text of the 1623 Folio on the right-hand page and a modernized version on the facing page.

The best guide to Shakespeare's sources remains Geoffrey Bullough's eight-volume compendium *Narrative and Dramatic Sources of Shakespeare* (1957–75). Volume IV (1962) provides substantial extracts from the major sources for *Henry V*, including a key dramatic source for *Henry V* and the preceding *Henry IV* plays, *The Famous Victories of Henry the fifth: Containing the Honourable Battell of Agin-court*. *Famous Victories* can also be found in *The Oldcastle Controversy* (1991) by Peter Corbin and Douglas Sedge. Anne Barton, in 'The King Disguised: Shakespeare's *Henry V* and the Comical History' (in *The Triple Bond: Plays, Mainly Shakespearean, in Performance* (1975), ed. Joseph G. Price, pp. 92–117), challenges Bullough's suggestion that the episode in which Henry dons Erpingham's cloak and moves among his troops in disguise is modelled on a passage in Tacitus' *Annals*.

Instead she proposes several historical romances if not as sources then as analogues for the encounter between the disguised king and three common soldiers. Shakespeare's principal historical source for the plays of the second tetralogy was the second edition of the multiply authored, multi-volume prose history commonly referred to as Raphael Holinshed's *Chronicles of England, Scotland, and Ireland* (1587). This vast work is available in a six-volume edition published in 1807–8. Alternatively, the Everyman edition (no. 800) compiled by Allardyce and Josephine Nicoll offers a single-volume abridgement that, on the whole, lives up to its title, *Holinshed's Chronicle, As Used in Shakespeare's Plays* (1927; repr. 1978). If neither is available a third, more selective compilation, *Shakespeare's Holinshed: An Edition of Holinshed's Chronicles, 1587; Source of Shakespeare's History Plays, King Lear, Cymbeline, and Macbeth* (1968), edited by Richard Hosley, provides much of the core material. Annabel Patterson's *Reading Holinshed's 'Chronicles'* (1994) reappraises Holinshed's *Chronicles* as 'an archive for cultural history . . . from which we might reconstruct the *conditions* of playwrighting' (p. xiii) in Shakespeare's time. The other chronicle history on which Shakespeare habitually relied, Edward Hall's *Union of the Two Noble and Illustre Families of Lancaster and York* (1548), is available as a Scolar Press reprint (1970).

BIBLIOGRAPHIES, ANTHOLOGIES AND COLLECTIONS

Richard Dutton provides a helpful survey of twentieth-century criticism of the second tetralogy in *Shakespeare: A Bibliographical Guide* (1990), edited by Stanley Wells.

Unfortunately, it was compiled before the ground shift in views on the first Quarto of *Henry V* had made itself felt, and it also unavoidably omits more recent work on the play's engagement with questions of national identity and the matter of Britain. *'Henry V': An Annotated Bibliography*, compiled by Joseph Candido and Charles R. Forker, is a valuable resource, but as it was published in 1983 it too has obvious limitations. Seventeenth- and eighteenth-century commentaries on *Henry V* can be found scattered across the six volumes of *Shakespeare: The Critical Heritage* (1974–81), edited by Brian Vickers. Useful collections of essays include *Shakespeare's Histories* (2004; ed. Emma Smith); *A Companion to Shakespeare's Works, Volume II: The Histories* (2003; ed. Richard Dutton and Jean E. Howard); *The Cambridge Companion to Shakespeare's History Plays* (2002; ed. Michael Hattaway); *Shakespeare's History Plays: Richard II to Henry V* (1992; ed. Graham Holderness); *William Shakespeare's 'Henry V'* (1988; ed. Harold Bloom); *Shakespeare: 'Henry V'* (1969; ed. Michael Quinn); *Twentieth-Century Interpretations of 'Henry V'* (1968; ed. Ronald Berman); and the journal *Shakespeare Survey 6* (1953) and *38* (1985).

TEXTUAL ISSUES

In recent years the status of the first Quarto of *Henry V* and its relationship to the first Folio version on which this edition and most other modern editions of the play are based have been the subject of renewed debate. At just over 1,620 lines, Q1 (1600) is half the length of F (1623), which at nearly 3,400 lines is one of Shakespeare's longest plays. Three influential theories have been advanced to explain the striking disparity between these two early versions of *Henry V*. The theory that Q1 represents an unauthorized 'bad' or 'pirated' text is set out by Alfred W. Pollard, in *Shakespeare Folios and Quartos: A Study in the Bibliography of Shakespeare's Plays 1594–1685* (1909), especially pp. 64–80. The theory that it is the product of a flawed attempt at 'memorial reconstruction' by two or more actors who had participated in performances of the 'long' version derives from W. W. Greg's *Shakespeare's 'Merry Wives of Windsor', 1602* (1910). It is most fully developed in relation to *Henry V* by George Ian Duthie, in 'The Quarto of Shakespeare's *Henry V*' (in *Papers Mainly Shakespearian* (1964), ed. Duthie). The favourite contenders for the role of 'memorial reporter' are the actors playing Exeter, Gower, the Governor of Harfleur and Scroop. The theory that it is a pared down acting version used by a reduced company of actors touring in the provinces has been elaborated most fully by Gary Taylor, in *Three Studies in the Text of 'Henry V'* (published with *Modernizing Shakespeare's Spelling* (1979) by Stanley Wells, pp. 37–164). This theory presupposes that the 'long' versions of the plays were performed substantially uncut in the London theatres. Kathleen Irace, in 'Reconstruction and Adaptation in Q *Henry V*' (in *Studies in Bibliography* 44 (1991), pp. 228–53), advocates elements of the second and third theories, arguing that the manuscript from which Q1 derives is a memorial reconstruction and was devised 'as a promptbook for use in performances outside London' (p. 249). Andrew Gurr, in *The First Quarto of 'King Henry V'* (2000), and Lukas Erne, in *Shakespeare as Literary Dramatist* (2003), have recently rejected all three theories. Gurr argues that Q1 represents 'a version closely based on the Shakespeare company's own performance script of the play, a text made for or from its first performances in 1599 . . . a text set from an authorised playhouse manuscript' (p. ix). Erne makes a similar claim, affirming that 'the authoritative performance script is what the first quarto imperfectly recovers' (p. 209). Far from being an unauthorized or 'pirated' version to be regarded with suspicion, Gurr characterizes Q1 as 'probably the best surviving example of a Shakespeare play-script as it was first performed by the company that bought it' (p. 2), a company for which Shakespeare acted and of which he was also a principal shareholder, having purchased a second share in the Lord Chamberlain's Men in 1599, the year in which *Henry V* was probably written. (Warren D. Smith, in 'The *Henry V* Choruses in the First Folio' (*Journal of English and Germanic Philology* 53 (1954), pp. 38–57), and David Bevington, in *Tudor Drama and Politics: A Critical Approach to Topical Meaning* (1968), argue for composition in 1600, but their arguments have attracted few adherents.) Annabel Patterson, in 'Back by Popular Demand: The Two Versions of *Henry V* ' (in *Shakespeare and the Popular Voice* (1989), pp. 71–92), argues that political developments, specifically the alarming deterioration in the already strained relations between Elizabeth and Essex after his unauthorized return from Ireland in September 1599, may account for the omission of the Chorus from Q1, as the thinly veiled reference to Essex in the fifth chorus and the Chorus's idolization of a popular military hero throughout may have been judged too dangerous to publish. The very fact that Q1 was rushed into print in August 1600 (a unique contraction of the usual two-to-three-year gap between the date a play was written by Shakespeare and first performed and the date a version came into print) may represent a 'tactical retreat' by the playing company in the very month Essex was to appear before the Privy Council to defend his conduct in Ireland.

Where most commentators characterize Q1 as more orthodox in its depiction of Henry V and his French campaign, Leah S. Marcus, in *Puzzling Shakespeare: Local Reading and Its Discontents* (1988), and Graham Holderness, in 'Writing and Fighting: *Henry V*' (in his *Textual Shakespeare* (2003), pp. 213–37), argue respectively that Q1 plebeianizes and carnivalizes the king. Q1 is not lesser or more orthodox; it is generically distinct. As Holderness puts it: 'The Henry of the Quarto is presented not as an epic hero or an awe-inspiring historical character, but as a "gentle gamester"' (p. 26). The validity of the theory of 'memorial reconstruction' and its application to the so-called 'bad' quartos, including Q1 of *Henry V*, has also been challenged by Paul Werstine, in 'A Century of "Bad"' Shakespeare Quartos' (*Shakespeare Quarterly*, 50 (1999), pp. 310–33), and Laurie Maguire, in *Shakespearean Suspect Texts: The 'Bad' Quartos and Their Contexts* (1996).

CRITICISM

No other Shakespeare play has divided modern critics as sharply as *Henry V* nor has any other Shakespearian character provoked such polarized responses as the victor at Agincourt. The case for Henry V as a Christian epic hero is put most famously by J. H. Walter in the introduction to his 1954 edition. John Dover Wilson also sturdily defends Henry V against his detractors in his introduction to his Cambridge edition (1947). The first person to publish the countervailing view of Henry as a warmongering tyrant appears to have been William Hazlitt in 1817, who memorably characterizes Henry V as 'a very amiable monster' (p. 170) in his *Characters of*

Shakespear[e]'s Plays (1949 edn). Dissatisfaction with the play, or more precisely with the 'long' Folio version, predates Hazlitt's attack on its hero (as the printing of the first Quarto in 1600 and a history of heavy revisions to the Folio text in performance from the time of its revival in the eighteenth century arguably attest). Writing half a century before Hazlitt, Samuel Johnson expressed bafflement that in the courtship scene 'Shakespeare now gives the king nearly such a character as he made him formerly ridicule in Percy'. To Johnson it appeared 'that the poet's matter failed him in the fifth act'. Although he had attempted 'to fill it up with whatever he could get', not even a writer as skilled as Shakespeare could 'paint upon vacuity'. As for the coarse sexual banter between Burgundy and Henry, 'the merriment is very gross, and the sentiments are very worthless' (*Notes to the Edition of Shakespeare's Plays*, quoted in *Samuel Johnson on Shakespeare*, ed. H. R. Woodhuysen (1989), p. 210). Unlike Johnson, it was not the abrupt shift from heroic drama to romantic comedy in the last act that concerned Hazlitt but rather Shakespeare's concerted effort (as he saw it) 'to apologize for the actions of the king', not least as Henry V 'seemed to have no idea of any rule of right or wrong, but brute force, glossed over with a little religious hypocrisy' (p. 168). Hazlitt never entertains the possibility that the play was designed to complicate, question or qualify a celebrated national legend.

The first essay to claim 'the play is ironic' was written by Gerald Gould in the aftermath of the First World War. The ironic interpretation of *Henry V* proposed by Gould in his ground-breaking essay 'A new reading of *Henry V*' (in *The English Review* 128 (1919), pp. 42–55; repr. abridged as 'Irony and Satire in *Henry V*' in *Shakespeare: 'Henry V'. A Casebook* (1969), ed. Michael

Quinn, pp. 81–94) has since become one of the dominant critical views of the play. Gould's ironic interpretation sharpens into a cynical view of Henry as 'too close for comfort to Machiavelli's ideal prince' in H. C. Goddard's *The Meaning of Shakespeare* (1951; vol. 1, p. 267), written in the aftermath of the Second World War. The appraisal of Henry V as a Machiavellian tyrant, ruthless, cunning and hypocritical, a master of verbal forms of deception, has been elaborated and variously embellished by a host of subsequent commentators, among them Andrew Gurr, in '*Henry V* and the Bees' Commonwealth' (*Shakespeare Survey 30* (1977), pp. 61–72), a particularly subtle variation on the standard approach; and Vicki Sullivan, in 'Princes to Act: Henry V as the Machiavellian Prince of Appearance' (*Shakespeare's Political Pageant: Essays in Literature and Politics* (1996), ed. Joseph Alulis and Vickie Sullivan).

Other commentators, such as Una Ellis-Fermor, in 'Shakespeare's Political Plays' (*The Frontiers of Drama* (1945; 2nd edn, 1948)), and Derek Traversi, in *Shakespeare: From 'Richard II' to 'Henry V'* (1957), are more equivocal. Ellis-Fermor supports the view that Henry V epitomizes Shakespeare's idea of the statesman-king. Henry V is 'the perfect public man' (p. 45); however, his political accomplishment is at the expense of the inner or 'private' person: 'It is in vain that we look for the personality of Henry behind the king; there is nothing else there ... There is no Henry, only a king' (pp. 45–6). According to Ellis-Fermor, this is why 'generations of Shakespeare's readers have found little to love in this play' (p. 46). Shakespeare's Henry V is 'a dead man walking' and 'Shakespeare himself ... begins to recoil' from the figure of the 'statesman-king' he had constructed across the *Henriad* with such care (p. 47). For Traversi, '*Henry V* represents ... a step in the realization of themes only fully developed in the tragedies' (p. 187). Henry's 'increasing awareness of his isolation' (p. 188), the elements of 'harshness and inhumanity' (p. 194) that accompany his exhibitions of self-control, and the notorious throat-cutting order are examples of 'the tougher strain of disillusioned realism that emerges from the play' (p. 194). In a seminal essay, 'Rabbits, Ducks and *Henry V*' (*Shakespeare Quarterly* 28 (1977), pp. 279–96; repr. as 'Either/Or: Responding to *Henry V*' in *Shakespeare and the Problem of Meaning* (1981)), Norman Rabkin compares Shakespeare's play to a gestalt sketch that can be perceived to be in the shape of either a rabbit or a duck with equal plausibility. For Rabkin, *Henry V* is a rabbit-duck, meaning that it can be interpreted by the audience as a heroic sequel to *Henry IV, Part I* that celebrates the victor at Agincourt as a 'mirror of all Christian kings' (II. Chorus.6) or as a sequel to the more troubling *Henry IV, Part II* that exposes the ruthlessness and hypocrisy of a Machiavellian opportunist. Its 'ultimate power', he argues, 'is precisely the fact that it points in two opposite directions, virtually daring us to choose one of the two opposed interpretations it requires of us' (p. 279). Where Rabkin argues that the opposing responses to *Henry V* tell us something about the play and about Shakespeare's own deep ambivalence, James Black, in 'Shakespeare's *Henry V* and the Dreams of History' (*English Studies in Canada* 1 (1975), pp. 13–30), and Alexander Leggatt, in *Shakespeare's Political Drama: The History Plays and the Roman Plays* (1988), argue that the critical and performance history of *Henry V* exposes, as no other Shakespearian drama, 'the biases of its interpreters' (p. 114).

Whether or not the critical divisions over *Henry V*

prompt commentators to reflect on their own interpretative practices, *Henry V* is a conspicuously self-reflexive drama. The self-conscious theatricality of the play and the self-conscious mastery of rhetoric exhibited by Hal-Henry-Harry across the *Henriad* are the subject of metadramatic studies by James L. Calderwood, *Metadrama in Shakespeare's Henriad* (1979); Joseph A. Porter, *The Drama of Speech Acts: Shakespeare's Lancastrian Tetralogy* (1979); John W. Blanpied, *Time and the Artist in Shakespeare's English Histories* (1983); and Kent T. van den Berg, *Playhouse and Cosmos: Shakespearean Theatre as Metaphor* (1985). Calderwood argues that 'in *Henry V* . . . the divinely guaranteed truths of Richard's reign and the ubiquitous lies of [Henry IV's] are succeeded by rhetoric, the language of conquest' (p. 7). However, where Calderwood finds that in Shakespeare 'Political affairs . . . become metaphors for arts' (p. 4), new historicist and cultural materialist critics argue the reverse. In his widely anthologized essay 'Invisible Bullets: Renaissance Authority and Its Subversion, *Henry IV* and *Henry V*' (*Political Shakespeare: New Essays in Cultural Materialism* (1985; 2nd edn, 1994), ed. Jonathan Dollimore and Alan Sinfield, pp. 18–47; repr. in revised form in *Shakespearean Negotiations: The Circulation of Social Energy in Renaissance England* (1988)), new historicist Stephen Greenblatt contends that 'Theatricality . . . is not set over against power but is one of power's essential modes' (p. 46). Although the play awakens 'subversive doubts' (p. 62), Greenblatt questions whether '*Henry V* can be successfully performed as subversive' (p. 63). 'The ideal king must be in large part the invention of the audience'; however, Greenblatt's totalizing assumption that all audience members will be 'induced to make up the difference, to invest in the illusion of magnificence'

(p. 63) is disputed by Jonathan Dollimore and Alan Sinfield, in 'History and Ideology: The Instance of *Henry V*' (*Alternative Shakespeares* (1985), ed. John Drakakis, pp. 206–27), and by Graham Bradshaw, who also takes issue with Dollimore and Sinfield's cultural materialist approach, in 'Is Shakespeare Evil?' and 'Being Oneself: New Historicists, Cultural Materialists, and *Henry V*' (*Misrepresentations: Shakespeare and the Materialists* (1993), pp. 1–33, 34–124). Other late-twentieth-century ideological readings include Leonard Tennenhouse, 'Strategies of State and Political Plays: *A Midsummer Night's Dream, Henry IV, Henry V, Henry VIII*' (*Political Shakespeare*, pp. 109–28); Gunter Walch, '*Henry V* as Working-House of Ideology' (*Shakespeare Survey 40* (1988), pp. 63–8); Robert Weimann, 'Bifold Authority in Shakespeare's Theatre' (*Shakespeare Quarterly 39* (1988), pp. 401–17); and Graham Holderness, *Shakespeare Recycled: The Making of Historical Drama* (1992) and '*Henry V*' (*Shakespeare: The Histories* (2000), pp. 136–55). Joel B. Altman, in '"Vile Participation": The Amplification of Violence in the Theatre of *Henry V*' (*Shakespeare Quarterly 42* (1991), pp. 1–32), argues that these recent ideological readings 'exult [ideological] process at the expense of play-wrighting', while formalists are hesitant to relate 'the play of significations in *Henry V* . . . to the shifting contours of the times' in which Shakespeare wrote. Both approaches tend 'to anaesthetize and immobilize . . . *Henry V*, arguably the most active dramatic experience Shakespeare ever offered his audience' (p. 2). In their place Altman provides an 'essentially rhetorical' reading of the play that explains 'the play's power in terms of its crafted interaction with the needs of its players and its first audiences' (p. 3). Describing *Henry V* as 'perhaps, Shakespeare's most conspicuous achievement in the reasoning *in utramque partem*' (p. 137), Paula Pugliatti, in *Shakespeare the Historian* (1996), relates the play's ambivalence to the rhetorical practice, central to the educational system of Shakespeare's day, of arguing on opposing sides of a question (*in utramque partem*). P. K. Ayers, in '"Fellows of Infinite Tongue": Henry V and the King's English' (*Studies in English Literature* 34 (1994), pp. 253–77), too favours a rhetorical approach and takes Henry's courtship of Katherine, specifically his spurious denial that he is one of 'these fellows of infinite tongue' (V.2.154–5), as the starting point for his investigation of 'the complex web of relationships between language and power' (p. 254) in *Henry V* and in the two parts of *Henry IV*.

Although numerous utterances in *Henry V* foreground the issue of gender, feminist studies of *Henry V* are comparatively thin on the ground, presumably because of the paucity of female roles in the play and in the second tetralogy as a whole. Lance Wilcox, in 'Katherine of France as Victim and Bride' (*Shakespeare Studies* 17 (1985), pp. 61–76), was the first to devote considered attention to the play's rape motif. Karen Newman, in 'Englishing the Other: "le tiers exclu" and Shakespeare's *Henry V*' (*Fashioning Femininity and English Renaissance Drama* (1991)), notes how 'the expansionist aims of the nation state are worked out on and through the woman's body' (p. 101) and includes a discussion of the Englishing of Katherine as a strategy of mastery. Peter Erickson, in 'Fathers, Sons, and Brothers in *Henry V*' (*Patriarchal Structures in Shakespeare's Drama* (1985; repr. in *William Shakespeare's 'Henry V'* (1988), ed. Harold Bloom, pp. 111–33)), traces the father–son motif and the damaging effect the martial definition of masculinity adopted by Henry V has on the play's comic denouement. Erickson's contention that 'The second tetralogy . . . avoids the threat to male rule that formidable women present in the first tetralogy by restricting women to the periphery' (p. 130) is endorsed by Jean E. Howard and Phyllis Rackin in *Engendering a Nation: A Feminist Account of Shakespeare's English Histories* (1997). In *Stages of History: Shakespeare's English Chronicles* (1990), Rackin emphasizes the resemblance between Henry V and Elizabeth I and explores Henry's reliance on women to legitimize his authority. In 'History and Ideology, Masculinity and Miscegenation: The Instance of *Henry V*' by Alan Sinfield with Jonathan Dollimore (*Faultlines: Cultural Materialism and the Politics of Dissident Reading* (1992) by Alan Sinfield, pp. 109–42; a revised, retitled and extended version of their essay in *Alternative Shakespeares* cited above), the authors argue that '[s]exualities and genders constitute a further ground of disturbance in the England of *Henry V*' (p. 127). '[B]anishment of the feminine and the female, even as these are conceived of by the masculine and the patriarchal, cannot easily be achieved' (p. 129): 'the state cannot be secured against female influence' (p. 139).

MILITARY CONTEXT

The battle between the genders tends not to be at the forefront of studies of Elizabethan militarism. Paul A. Jorgensen's landmark study *Shakespeare's Military World* (1956) remains an important guide to Shakespeare's knowledge of and extensive borrowings from sixteenth-century 'art of war' literature. J. Hale focuses on military character types in his essay 'Shakespeare and Warfare' (in *William Shakespeare: His World, His Work, His Influence*, ed. J. Andrews, 3 vols. (1985)). The field has since been enriched by two studies that depart from this earlier, characterological approach. In *Shakespeare's Theatre of War* (1998) Nick de Somogyi reads 'the Elizabethan plays of Shakespeare and his contemporaries in the light of contemporary writings which deal overtly with the waging, reporting, and social context of war' (p. 4). The twin aims of his study are to establish 'the aptness of the stage to the representation of war' (p. 4) and 'the currency of war among the audiences and players of London between 1585 and 1604' (p. 7), issues that bear directly on *Henry V* and its choruses. Nina Taunton is more concerned with the discourse of war as distinct from Somogyi's preoccupation with the theatricality of war in late-sixteenth-century England in *1590s Drama and Militarism: Portrayals of War in Marlowe, Chapman and Shakespeare's 'Henry V'* (2001). A limitation of her Foucauldian approach is that it tends to predetermine the ideological 'anxieties' found to be circulating in the war manuals and plays under examination. A compensatory strength of the book is its consideration of the challenge posed to the dominant, virulently masculinist conception of war by the historical presence of women in the military camp and on the battlefield, 'Officially excluded yet indubitably there' (p. 217). John Sutherland, in 'Henry V, War Criminal?' (*Henry V, War Criminal? And Other Shakespeare Puzzles* (2000) by John Sutherland and Cedric Watts), considers the twin possibilities that Henry's query after the battle of Agincourt, 'What prisoners *of good sort* are taken' (IV.8.74), means either that he was disobeyed at the height of the battle or that 'only the unregarded ordinary prisoners of war have been put to the sword', those of gentle rank having been retained for their ransom after giving their *parole* (p. 116). *Elizabeth I: War and Politics, 1588–1603* (1992) by the historian Wallace T. MacCaffrey provides an excellent account of the wider historical context of 1590s militarism and the factors that contributed to the eruption of open and sustained war in Ireland late in Elizabeth's reign.

NATION

Some of the best work on *Henry V* in recent years has been concerned with notions of nationhood and with the broader issue of how national identities are constituted in the play and over the history of its production. *Threshold of a Nation* (1979), Philip Edwards's ground-breaking study on the inter-relationship between imperialism and drama in the period, opened up this rich field of research. Subsequent studies have explored the play's engagement with Wales, Ireland and its treatment of the matter of Britain. Critics who have examined the preoccupation with Wales and Welsh identity in *Henry V* and in Shakespeare's English histories more generally include Lisa Hopkins, 'Welshness in Shakespeare's English Histories' (*Shakespeare's English History Plays: Performance, Translation and Adaptation in Britain and Abroad* (2004), ed. Ton Hoenselaars); Terence Hawkes, 'Bryn Glas' (*Shakespeare in the Present* (2002)); Patricia Parker, 'Uncertain Unions: Welsh Leeks in *Henry V*' (*British Identities and English Renaissance Literature* (2002), ed. David Baker and Willy Maley); and Megan S. Lloyd, *Speak It in Welsh: Wales and the Welsh Language in Shakespeare* (2007). David Cairns and Shaun Richards, in 'What Ish My Nation?' (in *Writing Ireland: Colonialism, Nationalism and Culture* (1988)), drew attention to a neglected aspect of Shakespearian drama that has since become a focus of scholarly interest. *Shakespeare and Ireland: History, Politics, Culture* (1997), edited by Mark

Thornton Burnett and Ramona Wray, includes impor-
tant essays on *Henry V* and Ireland by Lisa Hopkins,
'Neighbourhood in *Henry V*'; Willy Maley, 'Shakespeare,
Holinshed and Ireland: Resources and Con-texts'; and
Andrew Murphy, "Tish ill done: *Henry the Fift* and the
Politics of Editing'. The subject of David J. Baker's article
'"Wildehirissheman": Colonialist Representation in
Shakespeare's *Henry V*' (*English Literary Renaissance* 22
(1993), pp. 37–61) is aptly summarized in the title (see
also 'Imagining Britain: William Shakespeare's *Henry V*'
in his *Between Nations: Shakespeare, Spenser, Marvell, and
the Question of Britain* (1997)). Michael Neill, in 'Broken
English and Broken Irish: Nation, Language, and the
Optic of Power in Shakespeare's Histories' (*Shakespeare
Quarterly* 45 (1994), pp. 1–32; repr. in his *Putting History
to the Question: Power, Politics, and Society in English
Renaissance Drama* (2000)), discusses the disruptive
presence of the English enterprise in Ireland in
Shakespeare's history plays within a wider theatrical
context in which 'Ireland can seem to constitute . . . one
of the great and unexplained lacunae in the drama of the
period' (p. 11). In '"If the Cause be not good": *Henry V*
and Essex's Irish Campaign' (in his *Shakespeare, Spenser,
and the Crisis in Ireland* (1997)), Christopher Highley
argues that 'In *Henry V*, Shakespeare's misgivings about
Essex together with an awareness of burgeoning public
alarm at the war in Ireland produce a sceptical counter-
discourse about English expansionism within the British
Isles' (pp. 135–6). Philip Schwyzer sets out the case for
regarding *Henry V* as a play 'drenched in the now-familiar
language of British nationalism' (p. 128) with admirable
clarity in his chapter '"I am Welsh, you know": The
Nation in *Henry V*' (*Literature, Nationalism, and Memory
in Early Modern England and Wales* (2004)). Much

of Graham Holderness's '"What ish my nation?":
Shakespeare and National Identities' (*Textual Practice* 5
(1991), pp. 74–93; repr. in *Shakespeare's Histories* (2004),
ed. Emma Smith) is devoted to an examination of the
relationship between Laurence Olivier's and especially
Kenneth Branagh's iconic film adaptations of *Henry V*
and the patriotic and nationalist ideologies of 1940s and
1980s Britain respectively.

THE PLAY IN PERFORMANCE

A wide variety of resources are available to those inter-
ested in the performance history of *Henry V. Shakespeare
in Performance: Henry V* (1996) by James N. Loehlin and
King Henry V (2002) by Emma Smith are both excellent.
Anthony Brennan's *Henry V* (1992) includes a solid
chapter on its stage history. In his chapter on *Henry V* in
Shakespeare's Histories: Plays for the Stage (1964) Arthur
Colby Sprague appraises key trends in its performance
history from its revival in the eighteenth century through
to the early twentieth century, making his personal pref-
erences plain throughout. Several modern productions
benefit from publications that record aspects of the
production process by theatre and film professionals. *The
Royal Shakespeare Company's Production of 'Henry V' for
the Centenary Season at The Royal Shakespeare Theatre*
(1976) by Sally Beauman incorporates production photos,
costume sketches and numerous interviews with those
involved in the 1975 RSC production (dir. Terry Hands).
Written in the style of a diary, *English Shakespeare
Company: The Story of 'The Wars of the Roses', 1986–
1989* (1990) offers Michael Bogdanov's and Michael
Pennington's account of their touring production of the

two tetralogies. In his early autobiography, *Beginning* (1989), Kenneth Branagh comments extensively on the 1984 RSC production (dir. Adrian Noble), and on his own 1989 film version of *Henry V*, in both of which he played the title role. *'Henry V' at the National: A Rehearsal Diary* (2003), compiled by Peter Reynolds and Lee White, includes several photographs in its forty-four-page glimpse into the rehearsal process for the 2003 production (dir. Nicholas Hytner). The screenplay for Laurence Olivier's 1944 film can be accessed in *Henry V by William Shakespeare* (1984) in the Classic Film Scripts series. Branagh's *Henry V by William Shakespeare: A Screen Adaptation* (1989) includes a brief introduction by the actor-director together with an annotated version of the final edited film script (as distinct from the original screenplay) and numerous production stills. Other useful publications include Harry Geduld's *Filmguide to Henry V* (1976) on Olivier's 1944 film adaptation; Kenneth Branagh's essay on 'Henry V' in *Players of Shakespeare 2* (ed. Russell Jackson and Robert Smallwood; 1988); and Adrian Lester's on 'King Henry V' in *Players of Shakespeare 6* (ed. Robert Smallwood; 2004).

Laurence Olivier's film adaptation, *Henry V* (1944), Kenneth Branagh's 1989 film version and David Giles's 1979 BBC television film are all available on DVD. *The Wars of the Roses: Henry V* is a recording of a live performance of the English Shakespeare Company's touring production, directed by Michael Bogdanov (1997). The original soundtrack of Kenneth Branagh's film is also available, as is a sound recording of the unabridged New Cambridge Shakespeare text.

THE LIFE OF
HENRY THE FIFTH